"We all want to be heroes, but there are true limits to our activism. *The World Is Not Ours to Save* is a humbling reminder that we are free to love, serve and speak up because the greatest battles are not ours to win. This is an important read for young activists who seek to understand God's biblical vision for peace, justice and love on earth—while exploring their own role in the world. Through compelling historical and present-day narratives, Wigg-Stevenson casts a vision of activism that encourages us to think theologically about our activities and steward our calling, ultimately drawing us back to Jesus."

JENA LEE NARDELLA, cofounder and CEO, Blood:Water Mission

"Deeply personal, always fresh and to the point, and often funny, this book carries a wise and timely message. Wigg-Stevenson is both a voice to listen to and a leader to follow. I read the book with great profit."

OS GUINNESS, author, *A Free People's Suicide*

"If you are an activist inspired by the Christian faith and are experiencing a 'cause fatigue'— read this book! Tyler's beautifully written essay, theologically penetrating, wise and born out of his own experiences, will give you rest and help you not tire out of radical commitments and faith-based activism."

MIROSLAV VOLF, author, *A Public Faith*, Henry B. Wright Professor of Theology, Yale Divinity School, founding director, Yale Center for Faith and Culture

"*The World Is Not Ours to Save* is a bold and thorough exploration of Christian activism for the twenty-first century. Using rational biblical and theological reflection alongside heart-wrenching narrative and skillful juxtaposition, Tyler Wigg-Stevenson paints a descriptive landscape of the social, moral and ethical complexities of our time. The reader will be challenged to reach for a prophetic imagination and invited to live the way of peaceable action in a troubled and conflicted world."

PHILEENA HEUERTZ, founding partner of Gravity, A Center for Contemplative Activism, and author, *Pilgrimage of a Soul*

"I don't agree with Tyler Wigg-Stevenson on everything, but I always find him to be provocative, in the right sort of way. Tyler provokes thought and reflection, even from those who disagree, not simply the rattling of rival ideologies. Reading this book will prompt you to careful deliberation about what it means to love Christ and love neighbor. Even when you are on the opposite end of where Tyler comes down, you will be led to think through the issues in a fresh way. And that's a blessing."

RUSSELL D. MOORE, dean, Southern Baptist Theological Seminary

"There is a generation arising committed to reconciling Billy Graham's message of salvation with Dr. Martin Luther King's march for justice. Tyler Wigg-Stevenson embodies that mission and presents a practical framework for building a firewall against activism fatigue and cause-related myopia. In *The World Is Not Ours to Save*, Tyler submits the proposition that unbridled activism and advocacy results in a spiritual disbalance that merits a corrective prescription—one that emerges out of a kingdom lens and vocational discipline."

REV. SAMUEL RODRIGUEZ, president, National Hispanic Christian Leadership Conference, Hispanic Evangelical Association

"Anyone seeking to change the world? For the love of the planet and yourself—please read this book first. Mandatory navigation tools for the deep dive into social causes."

STEVE HAAS, chief catalyst, World Vision US

"Tyler's example of deep faith has given him the ability to engage a topic that most are overwhelmed by and helps us believe the seemingly impossible is quite possible. This book is one where love for God and people meet in a super inspiring way, and it leaves you believing the world can change."

LEROY BARBER, president, Mission Year, author, *Everyday Missions*

"God builds his kingdom, says Tyler Wigg-Stevenson. We don't. We can, however, dare to let God reveal his justice in our lives. The result is just as risky, but ultimately far more rewarding."

DAVID NEFF, editorial vice president of CT initiative development, Christianity Today Media Group

"Tyler's voice is deeply biblical, theological and ecclesial in an era of disastrous Christian shallowness in each of these critical arenas. Simultaneously majestic and hilarious, memoir and public ethic, *The World Is Not Ours to Save* is absolutely must-reading for any Christian who would seek to engage our broken world in the name of Jesus Christ."

DAVID P. GUSHEE, Director, Center for Theology and Public Life, Mercer University

"Tyler Wigg-Stevenson's *The World Is Not Ours to Save* is a must-read for anyone serious about understanding and ending the threat of nuclear weapons in our world today. As believers we are to be Christ, conscious of what a world with nuclear weapons and a world without them means to us socially, humanly and spiritually. The abolition of nuclear weapons is one of the most important issues we must pray for and take a stand on today."

JAESON MA, artist, musician and church planter

"*The World Is Not Ours to Save* walks Christ-followers through both his own journey and the story of Scripture, helping us arrive at a kind of world engagement and activism that is more effective than slogans and social media and more humane and healing than shouting down the world on cable news. This is a kind of activism that is drenched in the story of God and Christ's love for humankind. *The World Is Not Ours to Save* is a pilgrimage of the heart for those longing to see the fullness of God's kingdom."

SEAN PALMER, lead minister, The Vine Church, Temple, Texas

"I love Tyler. He has style, and wit, and innovation, and sass. I didn't like the title of the book. But then I read it. Tyler corrects some of the errors of activism and challenges the assumptions of belief-only Christianity. He reminds us here that works don't earn our salvation, but they do demonstrate it. And Tyler insists that we pray as if we depend on God, because we do . . . but that we also live as if God depends on us, because God does. May Tyler's words inspire us all to become the change we pray for."

SHANE CLAIBORNE, author, activist and lover of Jesus, www.thesimpleway.org

THE WORLD IS NOT OURS TO SAVE

FINDING THE FREEDOM TO DO GOOD

TYLER WIGG-STEVENSON

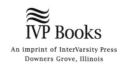

IVP Books

An imprint of InterVarsity Press
Downers Grove, Illinois

InterVarsity Press
P.O. Box 1400, Downers Grove, IL 60515-1426
World Wide Web: www.ivpress.com
E-mail: email@ivpress.com

InterVarsity Press® is the book-publishing division of InterVarsity Christian Fellowship/USA®, a movement of
students and faculty active on campus at hundreds of universities, colleges and schools of nursing in the United States
of America, and a member movement of the International Fellowship of Evangelical Students. For information about
local and regional activities, write Public Relations Dept., InterVarsity Christian Fellowship/USA, 6400 Schroeder
Rd., P.O. Box 7895, Madison, WI 53707-7895, or visit the IVCF website at <www.intervarsity.org>.

All Scripture quotations, unless otherwise indicated, are taken from the Holy Bible, New International Version®.
NIV®. Copyright ©1973, 1978, 1984 by International Bible Society. Used by permission of Zondervan Publishing
House. All rights reserved.

While all stories in this book are true, some names and identifying information in this book have been changed to
protect the privacy of the individuals involved.

Published in association with the literary agency of Wolgemuth & Associates.

Cover design: Cindy Kiple
Interior design: Beth Hagenberg
Images: man dragging globe: © robodread/iStockphoto
     arrows: © CHUTIMA CHOKKIJ/iStockphoto

ISBN 978-0-8308-3657-4

Printed in the United States of America ∞

Library of Congress Cataloging-in-Publication Data
A catalog record for this book is available from the Library of Congress.

P   22   21   20   19   18   17   16   15   14   13   12   11   10   9   8   7   6   5   4   3   2   1

Y   32   31   30   29   28   27   26   25   24   23   22   21   20   19   18   17   16   15   14   13

For Alan Cranston and John Stott,

whose going before has guided my way

CONTENTS

Part one

THE LIMITS OF ACTIVISM

1

THE WORLD IS NOT OURS TO SAVE

Thinking We Will Save the World

Contemporary critics of Christianity often ask what good the faith has done. I would introduce them to any one of the extraordinary believers I've come to know, whose faith compels them to work for myriad world-improving causes. Followers of Jesus, especially in the generation now coming of age, are near the heart of many places where the world shows signs of hope: clean water access, educational justice, HIV/AIDS treatment, creation care, poverty relief and development, microfinance, natural disaster response, post-conflict reconciliation, religious liberties, women's and children's welfare, and work to combat human trafficking, slavery and sexual exploitation and many, many more.

The activist spirit animating twenty-first-century Christianity is impossible to understand without the historical context of the previous generation's public engagement: that of the Religious Right and a more progressive wing typified by Jim Wallis's *Sojourners*, Ron Sider's Evangelicals for Social Action and Tony Campolo's Evangelical Association for the Promotion of Education. These groups broke with the preceding generation of evangelicals by living out their faith in the public arena, seeking systemic solutions to systemic problems, a move that has been embraced by the generation that has followed them. In the typology of cultural change described by sociologist James Davison Hunter, Christians have shifted decidedly in their cultural engagement from exclusively individualistic models like evangelism to include systems-based models like politics and social reform.[1] Current Christian efforts to help the poor, for example, are likely to demonstrate a simultaneous commitment to addressing poverty's root causes and providing direct aid to individuals and communities.

The current context of cultural and religious pluralism magnifies this development. After the disintegration of Christendom—a historical apparatus that gave cultural pride of place to Christianity—Christian truth claims cannot be taken for granted or simply asserted using logical apologetics. Rather, the truth of the faith appears to stand or fall based on its goodness, as shown in the lives of those who claim it. This means that Christianity has something to prove, and this in turn has generated a faith that is focused outward, engaged with culture, concerned with authenticity and activist in its orientation.

As a thirty-something, my hopes and fears for this generation are the hopes and fears I have for myself. Both hope and fear have been amplified with increased exposure to how I have seen us living out our faith. I believe that this generation bears extraordinary promise, but the fulfillment of this promise depends on our ability to confront our particular weaknesses. That is, the shift to systems thinking is not simply about having a more comprehensive perspective on complex phenomena like poverty and ecology. It also often means that we engage such issues in a way that presupposes that, or at least acts as if, the human condition can be fixed through human effort—that the world is ours to save. This is a problem.

The reasons this belief makes for a fragile spiritual foundation for world engagement are the central concern of this book. We are already seeing hairline fractures, like the "cause fatigue" I increasingly encounter among younger Christians. This doesn't mean there's something wrong with causes per se, but rather that we need a better way to engage them. We need a sense of enduring calling.

Christians heaven-bent on saving the world make me fear for the church of ten, twenty or thirty years from now—when, barring the Lord's return, the world is profoundly different than it is now but still irretrievably broken, violent and wicked. I wonder what will happen to us in the process.

Will zealous young Christians who are sold out for Christ eventually age out of faith-based activism, leaving our radical commitments for the safety of a private, middle-class "churchianity" that fits better with the demands of kids and family?

Will we go the other direction and reduce a gospel-proclaiming faith to its ethical and moral components, neglecting evangelism and sanctification in favor of a social program to which Jesus and the church are optional at best and superfluous at worst?

Will we suffer disillusionment and disappointment en masse, abandoning Christ in the process, as the passage of time relentlessly reveals to us that this will not be the generation specially equipped to solve the world's problems?

Will we respond to a calamitous event in a way that reveals that we have been rocky soil for the word of God, from which it blows away, rootless, during a time of testing?

I would not be surprised if future generations criticize ours along precisely such lines, though I hope they will be more merciful and charitable than we have often been with those who preceded us.

And yet none of these outcomes is a foregone conclusion. There is still a better way.

OCTOBER 3, 1999, SAN FRANCISCO

The Herbst Theater is a glittering wonder of gilt columns and crystal chandeliers and acres of red velvet. Eight giant beaux-arts murals by the Belgian artist Frank Brangwyn stretch to the soaring ceilings. A little more than a half century earlier, when the world was still convulsed in war, representatives from fifty nations gathered in this very room to sign the United Nations Charter. San Francisco's majestic city hall sits directly across the street. If you could bottle elegance and sell it, it would smell like this place. In sum, it is not a venue you might associate with the act of getting naked.

But tonight you would be wrong, because there are fifty-odd people disrobing outside the dignified foyer. They march out onto Van Ness Avenue and begin their chant: "Nudes, not nukes!" The following day, the brief *San Francisco Examiner* story about the protests would wryly note that, "The night air was chilly enough to have a noticeable effect on some participants."

I am there too—the only representative of the organization hosting the event—fully clothed, rooted to the spot and sporting a suit and tie and a look of utter, slack-jawed horror.

In a little under twenty-four hours, I would hear the voice of God. But I didn't know that yet. I was simply convinced that I faced arrest for inadvertently presiding over an act of mass public indecency.

Each of us has his own road to the foot of the cross, and I suppose that a naked anti-nuclear protest in San Francisco is no more or less worthy than any other mile marker. The particular leg of the journey that led to this night, however, is just as odd as the evening itself.

HOW I LEARNED TO HATE THE BOMB

My path to the Herbst Theater that night had begun four months prior, on Memorial Day, the day I graduated from Swarthmore College. I had majored in religious studies, though I had no religion

myself. Nor did I have a job lined up. After the commencement ceremony, I fell to talking with the father of a classmate. He told me I
needed to go work for Alan Cranston, the retired US senator from
California. "Doing what?" I asked. "Eliminating nuclear weapons"
was his answer. A month and three thousand miles later, I crossed
the Bay Bridge into San Francisco to start my new job.

Alan, who insisted on the informality of first names, was an extraordinary man. As a young journalist in Europe before World War
II, he had witnessed the rising menace of Nazism. So, when he saw
how the official English-language edition of *Mein Kampf* had been
sanitized of much of its anti-Semitism, Alan translated and published a complete and annotated version to expose the führer—a
project that came to a halt only when Hitler sued him for copyright
violation in a Connecticut court.

After the war, Alan entered politics, and in 1968 he was elected as
one of California's senators. He served the state for four terms, until
1992, in the process rising to the position of Democratic whip and
running in the 1984 presidential primaries. During the Cold War, he
became a forceful critic of nuclear dangers and the arms race with
the Soviet Union—a position bolstered by his equally vigorous advocacy on behalf of soldiers as the top Democrat in the Committee
on Veterans' Affairs. Utterly convinced of the evil of nuclear weapons,
he dedicated his considerable energies in his post-Senate retirement
to their global abolition.

The ambitiously named Nuclear Weapons Elimination Initiative
was three people: Alan and me and Zack Allen, a year older than me
and fresh out of Stanford. Alan worked from his home in the South
Bay hills. Zack and I worked from the most splendid office I will ever
hope to occupy: the former Coast Guard commandant's house, converted into office space and separated from the San Francisco Bay by
fifty feet of sand beach.

Glorious location aside, this was a hard season. San Francisco boomed with dot-com fever, so I couldn't find or afford an apartment. For several weeks, I slept under my office desk clandestinely. This arrangement ended abruptly when a cleaning lady and I scared each other half to death, and the office manager told me, not unkindly, that I needed to make other arrangements.

I had little money and fewer friends, so I worked all the time. I became immersed in nuclear weapons. I learned that the threat had not gone away with the Cold War's end. Especially chilling was the knowledge that the United States and Russia maintained their intercontinental ballistic missiles (ICBM) on high-alert launch status and that these systems were far from foolproof. Given that one side's ICBM takes about fifteen minutes to reach the other's territory and that a counterattack would be ordered on detection of a launch, this meant that an invisible thirty-minute countdown clock hung permanently over the world. My new awareness haunted my every waking minute and probably explains a good deal about my social life at the time. I was not, you might say, the life of the party.

THE VOICE IN THE STAIRWELL

The night of the naked protest happened about three months into my job. We had convened a public panel discussion about nuclear dangers, in the splendor of the Herbst Theater, unaware of the backdrop we were setting for the incipient nude tableau. My boss, the senator, shared the stage with some other anti-nuclear advocates of a decidedly more flamboyant stripe. Among them were Patch Adams, the physician/clown depicted by Robin Williams in the eponymous film, and Dr. Helen Caldicott, an Australian physician and famous activist. I think Alan made his remarks, and then Dr. Caldicott and then Patch Adams took the podium.

As I watched the episode unfold, I had no idea it was setting the stage for a life-changing event. Patch Adams got up and asked the audience how much they really cared. "What are you willing to do," he roars in my memory, "to get rid of nuclear weapons? Would you—" he pauses for effect, "take off all your clothes and march in the street?"

Let's assess the scene. I've spoken to literally thousands of people about nuclear weapons in recent years, most of the time in churches, and I can say with some certainty that this line would not go over well in 99.9 percent of venues. But a (1) free (2) public forum (3) about nuclear weapons (4) on a school night (5) in San Francisco (6) ten years after the end of the Cold War involves the other 0.01 percent, because the room is full of unreconstructed hippies. Perhaps they have been walking around for decades with a tiny itch in the backs of their skulls—an amorphous longing, an unarticulated need.

This evening, Patch Adams has given their inchoate desire a name and direction: they want to get naked, meaningfully. It has been so long since anyone asked them to. Would they? Just try to stop them. Hands move toward the hems of ponchos; fingers twitch around toggles on Guatemalan vests. And then, like a horrified Moses, I stand in the back while a pink sea parts around me and makes a jubilant exodus into the wilderness of San Francisco.

That's really how the story of that evening ends. We whisked my boss out the back; senators, even in retirement, are not hugely partial to being associated with naked protests. Unsurprisingly, the White House did not dispatch a special envoy to San Francisco to let us know that the nude march had prompted an emergency disarmament summit with the Russians. Nothing happened. The police ignored the event. A reporter or two filed a bemused report. And that was that.

Often it is the questions you are asked, however, not the answers you are given, that prove most important in the long term. The day after the naked march, I was running around doing my other jobs for the conference. But I couldn't get Patch Adams out of my head. *What would you be willing to do to get rid of nuclear weapons?*

If you have ever been twenty-two and passionate about a cause, you know the answer to this one: anything. You would do anything. Visions of dramatic, world-saving actions filled my mind: a hunger strike in front of the White House or chaining myself to the fence of a nuclear base. But as my imagination played out these scenarios, I quickly saw their vanity. They would accomplish no more than the ludicrous (albeit brave) protest of the prior evening. My daydreams moved on to less ostentatious ambitions, like just showing up to labor against nuclear weapons every day for the rest of my life. But this vision, albeit more longsuffering, led to the same place: the nuclear weapons system could smile and swallow my sacrifice as if nothing had ever happened.

It hit me as I walked briskly down a hallway on the mezzanine level at the south side of the Fairmont Hotel: I was *willing* to do anything. But there was nothing I *could* do. This realization dropped me midstride. I saw a service stairwell to my right, slipped inside and crumpled onto the rough concrete stair. And I wept in despair for the world I so desperately wanted to save from itself.

Then, for the first—and, to date, the clearest—time in my life, I heard the voice of God.

God said, *The world is not yours, not to save or to damn. Only serve the one whose it is.*

I walked out of the stairwell with a wet face and a peaceful heart.

FOUNDING TWO FUTURES

In the more than a decade that has passed since that day, I have become an insider practitioner in the world of Christian activism and an eyewitness to the hopes, fears and passions that mark a rising generation of would-be world changers. This book emerges from that vantage point. For this reason, it is a deeply personal book as well: the criticisms I level find their first target in my own work and tendencies, and the hopes I articulate for faithful Christian work and witness are those I aspire to.

The path that I took out of that stairwell in the Fairmont Hotel led me eventually to seminary and ordained ministry. That's another, longer story. But even as my commitment to the elimination of nuclear weapons was transformed by my emerging faith, I never left the cause altogether. And, in early 2007, when an old friend from the disarmament community phoned to ask whether I could help bridge the divide between nuclear security and religious communities, I discerned a call from God to return and give all my attention and energy to that issue.

The result was an experimental outreach to Christians on the dangers of nuclear weapons in the twenty-first century, focusing primarily but not exclusively on theologically and politically conservative, evangelically minded Protestants—that is, the types of Christians who are not known for their participation in "Ban the Bomb" campaigns. Our goal was to get the threat and evil of nuclear weapons back on the church's radar and thus to create a morally grounded, nonpartisan body of believers who could act faithfully and create constructive change. After a couple years of behind-the-scenes outreach to key Christian leaders, the Two Futures Project (2FP) debuted as a public cause in 2009.

I believe that this movement's work has helped to focus new attention on nuclear weapons as a matter of faith. Stories about evangelicals against the Bomb have appeared in national and regional media, both Christian and secular, in print, television and radio. *Relevant* magazine's tenth anniversary issue cited our work as one of the top fifty ideas to emerge since they began publication. Major

Christian conferences like Q, Jubilee and Catalyst have featured 2FP's work. In 2011, the board of directors of the National Association of Evangelicals, representing more than forty-five thousand churches and tens of millions of American Christians, voted without objection to adopt a new policy position on nuclear weapons, reflecting the types of concerns 2FP has focused on. The World Evangelical Alliance, representing more than 600 million Christians in 129 national alliances worldwide, has engaged the issue by forming the Global Task Force on Nuclear Weapons. With similarly renewed attention to nuclear weapons in mainline Protestant and Roman Catholic circles, I believe that Christians are moving as one in the right direction and that the issue is with us to stay.

The work has been challenging and often exhausting, but immensely gratifying as well. One of the things for which I am most personally grateful has been the way that 2FP has opened the doors for me to encounter a generation of Christians that is passionately committed to living their faith in every part of their lives, working to do good and alleviate suffering in a huge variety of issues.

But younger Christians at the start of the twenty-first century aren't special. We get some things right, and we get a lot of things wrong, just like those who came before us and just like those who will follow us. This means we are called to a task that is at once as particular as our historical situation and as common as the sinful condition from which every follower of God is redeemed.

SEEKING FIDELITY

The question to us is, simply, how can we seek the particular shape of faithfulness in the time and place that God has called us into being and over which God has given us the privilege of stewardship? This book is an attempt to address that question in two parts.

The first begins with this chapter's diagnosis of the potential dangers in the activist sensibility currently on the rise within the church. It then critiques four tendencies that I often see at work in Christian efforts to save the world—including my own.

First, we get our *calling* wrong when we imagine that God needs us, to be the hero of our own story, rather than Christ (chapter two). Second, we routinely misdiagnose the *problem of our world*, underestimating the brokenness of sin and overestimating our ability to fix things (chapter three). Third, our *witness of God* often depicts a Lord who is domesticated to serve our causes (chapter four). Fourth, a justifiable focus on external problems can easily blind us to the depth of our complicity in the pain of *the human condition* (chapter five).

I know these errors intimately because I have personally stumbled on every one. The problem with such tendencies is not that they make us into activists, because there is nothing wrong (and there is often a great deal of good) with being an activist. Rather, the problem is that they make us into *bad* activists. They do not offer an accurate depiction of our callings, our world, our God or our condition. As such, they set up a false understanding of reality, leading in turn to bad theology, bad practices, bad activism. This results in discouragement, burnout and cause fatigue.

The second half of the book builds a constructive alternative that unfolds in precisely the opposite order from the critique: human condition, God, world and calling. It begins with *God's kingdom of peace as the solution to the human condition*, as articulated in Micah 4:1-5 (chapter six). This commitment to comprehensive peace seems to be a natural next step for a church community that has rediscovered justice as a core value of Christian life.

Then, digging deeper into Micah's vision, we explore his description of *peace with God*, as seen through worship, discipleship and evangelism (chapter seven). Next we look at Micah's depiction of *peace among the nations*, which entails justice, industry and nonaggression (chapter eight). Third, we see that Micah's *peace in community* is marked by dignity, prosperity and security (chapter nine). We conclude in chapter ten with a two-part proposal. First: that a spiritually faithful and pragmatically sustainable activism must be seen through the limiting lens of vocation, or calling. And second: a new vision for the shape of Christian activism, in light of this vocational focus.

In closing, two caveats. First, my obsessive insistence that we cannot fix the world may sound to some readers like an exhortation to passivity, do-nothingism, cultural retreat or despair. Nothing could be further from my intention. I write this book as one who began his Christian journey as an activist and who has remained an activist while walking the paths of discipleship and ordained ministry. I applaud the millions of Christians whose daily, loving labor makes an invisible God visible to a broken and sinful world, and I offer this book with the hope that it will encourage their continued service.

Moreover, though my reading of Scripture sees the kingdom as something that God alone will bring—rather than a world order that we can gradually build—I totally disavow any end-times theologies that treat the world as a disposable quantity to be used and abused. I have no desire to return to the branches of Christianity that saw efforts of social reform as little more than "rearranging deck chairs on the Titanic." There is no contradiction in laboring as Christians to serve the kingdom that is "at hand" and "near to us" while believing that such efforts are distinct from its final consummation.

In fact, I see this understanding as encouraging activist freedom, which is the point of this book: because we know that the work is *God's* to bring about, we can labor without the anxiety of imagining that the welfare of history rises or ebbs on the tide of our own blood, sweat and tears. And we can rejoice at those foretastes of the kingdom that we are privileged to behold in our own time.

Second, this book is an unfolding answer to an open-ended question: how can a results-minded Christian best seek the kingdom of God? As such, it demonstrates the character of wandering more than it does a tried-and-true recipe for getting discipleship right. The vision of the narrow road, whose fruits I have seen in the lives of elder saints, inspires me to inhabit the lifelong calling of dying daily to sin and rising in Christ and thereby seeking to embody God's will on our patch of earth as it is through the whole expanse of heaven. This is a story about not saving the world.

DON'T BE A HERO

Getting Ahead of Our Calling

Nobody spends time working to make a difference that doesn't matter. To the contrary, Christian activists past and present have tackled some of the world's biggest problems. In our drive to accomplish great things, it's easy to get caught up in the idea that we're called to be heroes. But such a vision misses three things that will undermine us at every step.

The first is the way in which our love of heroes can subtly celebrate our fallen condition rather than grieve over it. This leads to the second mistake: our personal discipleship as followers of Christ can take second place to making a bigger impact for our causes. Third, a heroic calling puts us and our concerns at the center of history, when we are actually all minor characters populating the salvation drama centered around Jesus Christ.

EGG

My mother held me fast to her side as I stared over the balcony rail and she let the egg drop. Then we trooped down three flights of stairs to inspect the white and yellow mess splattered across the driveway.

"This is what could happen to you," she told me, as I crouched to inspect the broken remains, "if you keep trying to fly." I took in her words in silence, a tiny, serious figure sporting red underpants and socks over blue pajamas, my homemade cape brushing the ground.

Today my mother cringes to tell this story. She worries that it might have been a bit much for a young child to take in, and she laments a first-time mom treating her three-year-old like a rational adult. Her concern was well founded, however, because I was a stickler for realism when it came to my Halloween costumes. My second Halloween I groused about the mismatch between my rabbit outfit and my all-too-human hands, until my mom finally stuck tube socks on my hands. Content that my costume was at last complete, I sat in my head-to-toe white fleece, pouring sweat, happily struggling to turn the pages of my books with my smooth cotton paws.

I had become a danger to myself, therefore, with the combination of a growing ability to climb and a Superman costume that I preferred over normal clothing. Our house was almost laughably un-child-friendly: a rambling three-story affair clinging to a hillside in Laguna Beach, with a little pond for me to drown in and seemingly limitless ledges from which I could leap to my death. Flushed with the discovery of my first superhero, I would fly, cape streaming, off the back of the couch, off the high hearth and off anything else I could climb.

As every kid understands, Superman offered heroism—an attribute notably deficient in my previous costumes. My Superman outfit came with a purpose that practically demanded an endless reservoir of dramatic gestures: a messiah flinging himself from untold heights to right wrongs below. Superman *saved* things.

So it should have been no surprise that my mother, growing more and more petrified by shouting leaps followed by increasingly loud thuds, took an egg in one hand and me in the other up to the balcony for a bit of performance-art-as-discipline.

We never did clean that egg up. Like a crucified criminal in ancient Rome, the corpse of the egg simply desiccated where it lay—a warning to passers-by, a grim reminder of our standing under powers greater than us. Afterward, I would point at it as we came and went, each time pronouncing a somber eulogy, "Egg." Thus I received one of my first lessons in limitations.

It didn't stick.

LOVING THE FALL

As we age, we begin to realize that the world is not exactly the way it's supposed to be. Our parents tell us not to play in the street or touch the oven or run away in the grocery store. Such boundaries teach us that existence is unavoidably dangerous. We also acquire the sense that this danger, the inherent vulnerability of life, is morally charged. There are good guys and there are bad guys, and we should avoid the bad guys. So we don't talk to strangers or get in cars with people we don't know.

I suspect that it's this very recognition that makes us fall in love with superheroes the way we do. How could we not? On the one hand, here's a world that we're discovering is broken and fraught. And on the other, here are these characters who are super-empowered to do something to fix the big problems. They can swoop into a hopeless situation and make it right.

These superhero ambitions are a funny kind of fantasy, though. As children confronted by the world's fallenness, we rarely seem to dream up a different kind of world, one where there aren't any problems. We usually dream up a different kind of me—a hero who's up to the challenge of confronting it. That's interesting, isn't it? There's no particular reason why, when we meet a situation that seems daunting, we shouldn't simply wish for the challenge to go away. But kids seem to prefer imagining a way to defeat it instead.

A few years back, someone who didn't know me very well suggested that I might enjoy John Eldredge's *Wild at Heart*, a sort of manual for masculine Christianity. The premise of the book is that "in the heart of every man is a desperate desire for a battle to fight, an adventure to live, and a beauty to rescue." I think the assumed gender roles in this are mostly nonsensical and sad: our friends' sons and daughters alike range in demeanor from St. Francis to Genghis Khan, and the idea that all girls are wilting damsels and all boys triumphant warriors leaves out a lot of people. But Eldredge might be right about the fact that people often have an intrinsic, desperate desire for battle.

I am ambivalent about this. In part, I have to think that our inclination toward conflict can serve the good, because the world is fallen and life is hard. As we read in Paul's letter to the Ephesian church, our adversaries are not simply our own weak flesh and blood but spiritual "powers and principalities" that struggle against us (Ephesians 6:12 KJV). That's why Paul talked about every follower of Christ putting on the armor of faith. Hero stories—from ancient mythology to modern comics—give girls and boys a sense of courage and self-sacrifice. They help us understand the struggle of living in a fallen world, and they magnify what it means to be virtuous in that context. We need heroes because the world is the way it is, and heroes give us examples of how to live in it with grace, persistence and nobility.

But our heroic impulse also reveals something dark and sinister about human nature. After all, superheroes require supervillains. They're nothing without them. Imagine Superman in a world without Lex Luthor and kryptonite. He just goes about normal business, flying to and from the grocery store, cooking up his Swanson dinner with heat vision, using his X-ray vision to see whether the mail has come yet. He irons his cape. He composts.

In other words, Superman minus villains equals boring.

Superman, Batman and Spider-Man are *crimefighters*. They're not defined by what they're for, but what they're against. True, Superman is about "truth, justice and the American way." But that doesn't require superpowers unless someone is threatening those ideals. Superheroes are who they are because they're in the struggle, in the combat. They depend on their opponents for their existence. If crime stopped, what would superheroes fight? Who would they be? They'd just be a bunch of strong, smart guys in oddly tight outfits moping around with nothing to do.

This means that there's something in our love of heroism that also must love, in a strange and hidden way, everything that heroes fight against—the villain, the evil adversary. The adversary makes the hero the hero. It's the adversary who lets us fight.

I've reflected a great deal about this as someone whose life work is primarily negative in orientation. For much of my adult life, I have woken up every day thinking about a problem: how to ensure that nuclear weapons are never again used and that they are eventually abolished. I hope that my motives for doing this are mostly pure. But there's definitely some part of me that loves the war of it, too, the excitement and the scale.

I know I'm not alone. The nonprofit world mostly deals with problems that need fixing, and those of us in the field talk a good game about wanting to work ourselves out of a job. Most of this is true; my friends who work in humanitarian fields are high-minded and care about others. But I suspect that a lot of them, like me, also secretly love the sense that they're stepping into the ring and popping the devil in the jaw. This is a dangerous desire to indulge.

In Sebastian Junger's superb book *War,* which chronicles a year he spent in Afghanistan's Korengal Valley with the US Army's Second Platoon, Bravo Company, he describes how the men grew to crave the excitement of firefights. Perched in the most dangerous outpost at the edge of the most dangerous valley in one of the world's most dangerous countries, the troops didn't have much to do but eat poorly, sleep anxiously and fight like hell.

When days or weeks went by without enemy contact, the men started to go stir crazy, and tension rose in the camp. They had become addicted to the thrill of combat, and normal life just didn't cut it anymore. Things only got worse when the men tried to reenter the banalities of civilian existence. A lot of them couldn't take it and found their way back to a combat deployment as quickly as they could. They'd gotten to the point of needing an enemy.

In a strange way, to accept evil as our opponent is to affirm it. This forecloses the possibility of imagining the holy alternative, where evil is not fought because it *does not even exist*. Finding ourselves in an arena with evil, we happily draw our swords and wade into the fight. But this means fighting on the devil's own terms, accepting the boundaries he has drawn for our gladiatorial arena. Loving the fight with sin means loving sin itself. It means that you can't want to win. What would you do if you did?

And yet we cannot be indifferent to evil. So how do we hate evil the way that God would have us do? The answer is the acceptance of Jesus' astonishing declaration about the crucifixion: "It is finished" (John 19:30). God has "disarmed the powers and authorities [and] made a public spectacle of them, triumphing over them by the cross" (Colossians 2:15).

Such claims can be difficult to believe—just look at the world! The powers and authorities of evil seem well armed, and the battle seems far from over. This is why faith in the cross of Christ is precisely that: *faith* that the moral pivot of history was a hill in an insignificant corner of the Roman Empire two thousand years ago. It requires faith to believe that all the heroism the universe could need was exercised there, in one man dying for the sin of the entire cosmos (John 1:29). In that very faith, we can see that the Lord does not call us to be heroes fighting evil, but to love the one who has already defeated it.

THE BBs IN THE COAT CLOSET

I learned my lesson in limitations—and gravity—with the egg off the balcony. But the urge to be Superman, to save the world, only got stronger. This did not make my childhood unique. In most respects, I suppose I grew up like many other children of the eighties in suburban Southern California. We went to the beach and had taco night and lived in a stucco house with a sycamore tree in the front yard. What made my house and family different from those of my friends, though, were the BBs—the copper-coated ammunition for an air gun—that we kept in our closet. When it came to world saving, those BBs gave me a sense of the stakes.

You see, my parents had alter egos. By day they worked normal jobs as a computer programmer and a public school teacher. But in the evenings, our house hosted meetings of the anti-nuclear group with which they were passionately and deeply involved. I remember meeting nights with great pleasure, because I got to watch TV with my dinner (an otherwise taboo practice in our house) and eat Kraft mac and cheese. I can still clearly recall the sounds and smells of those evenings: the muffled pitch of people greeting one another as they arrived; coffee burbling in the big percolator; the easel and flip charts and permanent markers; the comforting murmur of grownup voices through the den wall.

My parents weren't the sort of activists who held picket signs and shouted slogans. Instead, their group focused on public education about the dangers of the nuclear arms race in the 1980s and about the need to pursue alternative solutions to conflict. So they'd go around to schools and community centers and talk with other concerned citizens. That's where the BBs came in. They were part of a teaching exercise used to demonstrate the insane firepower of the global nuclear arsenal.

To do the exercise, you needed a couple thousand of the little pellets and a small steel trash can. You'd take a single BB, tiny and hard to grasp, and you'd say, "This one BB represents the power of the first atomic bomb, dropped on Hiroshima in 1945, which killed more than one hundred thousand people." Then you'd drop the BB in the trash can with a sharp, resounding *ping*. And then you take your Tupperware full of thousands of BBs and say, "This represents the total destructive power of all the nuclear weapons we have today," and pour it slowly into the can. It was deafening and took forever. People winced throughout the whole thing, and afterward everyone in the room sat under a sort of stunned hush.

The BBs are emblematic of the conceptual juxtapositions that made up my happy and essentially ordinary childhood: this illustration of humanity's capacity for global suicide sat in the hall closet, next to the jackets and my boogie board. In my childish perception, I knew that nuclear weapons were bad and that they would kill a lot of people—maybe everyone—if ever used. I knew that the arms race was also bad and that our political leaders were risking everything in a showdown with the USSR. I knew that we had more in common with the Russians than most people thought and that the path to peace ran through a better understanding of our shared humanity.

Above all, I knew that the world needed to be saved from itself and that this undertaking was the core of a meaningful life.

My family never went to church, and I had a decidedly irreligious upbringing; Christian faith came later to me. However, I was taught that the privilege of my stable family, solid middle-class status and education were an investment in me that demanded a return for the betterment of society. The much-repeated maxim "To whom much is given, much is expected" could have hung over my upbringing like the slogan over a heraldic crest. But, tellingly, I knew it only as a personal motto of President Kennedy—not as the words of Jesus recorded in the Gospel of Luke. With this formulation, it seemed to me that the world just needed enough people with decent educations, good work ethics and reasonable goodwill. How hard could it be?

THE ANGRIEST ACTIVIST

At one point, I was involved with an organization that had the grand mission of tackling the world's biggest problems. The leader of the organization—I'll call him Bill—had a Rolodex full of contact information for top leaders around the world in government, business, civil society, religion, arts, entertainment. He had built his connections on the strength of his charisma and his genuine desire to do good in a world plagued with problems. Everyone who met him came away with the impression of a charming, sincere leader— a not-for-profit hero who was doing great things.

When you got a little closer, however, cracks in this world-saving image started to appear. Bill was great in a public setting, where he could communicate his vision with grand, heartfelt rhetoric. But out of the public view, away from anyone he needed to impress, his personality became far more brittle. He flew into rages at small obstacles and stalked through the office wearing an invisible bubble of cold anger, chewing out junior staff for minor mistakes or differences in opinions. This anger had led to repeated complete staff turnovers. Most tellingly, over several months, the staff saw him grow increasingly abusive, especially to another organizational executive who had come on board to help stabilize operations. There seemed to be a huge disconnect between his vision for the world and the way he treated those around him.

Bill is an extreme example, but I frequently come across this personality type in activist settings: men and women whose good intentions and grand ambitions blind them to the terrible ways they interact with real human beings, including their coworkers and family. You'll find leaders who love a concept—peace, community, flourishing and so on—but don't seem to like people very much.

I get this, because people are a lot easier to love in the abstract than we are in person. But you have to wonder about activists who almost seem to wish that everyone would just get out of the way so they can get on with building a good society. Such leaders often wind up sitting in the rubble of their ambitions, having burned through all their relationships—left alone with a great vision for what the world could look like if God were to call and ask for their help.

Christians are not immune to this trait. If anything, we can be more susceptible to the lure of our own grand plans, because they're ostensibly in the service of God and his kingdom. I suspect that each of us knows a Christian leader or two who was possessed by a vision to do this or that great deed for Jesus, but whose personal character, conduct and sense of self made us wonder who he or she was taking orders from.

Our job is not to judge, for in judging others we submit ourselves to the same scrupulous measure. I can see these tendencies in activists like Bill, because I know them so well in my own heart. My intimate familiarity with the siren song of ambition is what makes me so concerned about much of the talk I hear in Christian circles today. Everywhere I go, it seems that people are talking about saving or changing the world. The message to individuals is that we should be leaders—heroes—who can make an impact.

But *impact* is value neutral. It's a concept based on degree of influence rather than quality. If I make an impact on something, all I've done is hit it really hard—with no guarantee that it's better for the collision.

In my own organizational planning and in Christian circles more broadly, I have found that it is easy to be inadequately self-critical about our desire to make an impact because we know up front that we're doing it for Jesus and the kingdom of God. We're justified by our motivations. However, even a brief glance at the checkered history of the church suggests the worthiness of some introspection about merely "making a difference" for the Lord. The Crusades and the Inquisition hit pretty hard in the name of Jesus. But did they do him good? Or did they bring disrepute to his name and his mission?

I fear that our faith easily becomes imbalanced in its outward focus toward "activist" or "missional" goals. Activism and mission are necessary and good, and they can and should be directed toward formation in Christlikeness. But in practice these goals readily and frequently become ends in themselves. If we accomplish great things in Jesus' name, but do so while becoming less and less like him, then God will use our deeds in spite of who we are—rather than through who we are. Also, a Christianity that exalts heroes and grand accomplishments can discourage many people who may not feel like their gifts are significant enough to offer. But the church, like a living body, needs all its members.

To avoid becoming like Bill will require that we continually test our entire lives against the witness of the Spirit in Scripture. Are our plans conducive to the continued ripening of the fruit of the Holy Spirit in our lives: love, joy, peace, patience, kindness, goodness, faithfulness, gentleness and self-control (Galatians 5:22-23)? Or do we find ourselves justifying the sacrifice of "minor" personal virtues in the name of the major public goods that we hope to accomplish, such as getting angry because others are not accomplishing tasks as readily as we would like or living in anxiety about attaining certain outcomes?

We should remember that God does not need our big plans. Instead, he calls us to become little Christs. So perhaps we would do well to pump the brakes of ambition, to slow down a bit while we discern whether we are moving in the right direction. After all, if we are headed the wrong way, it would be much better to be moving slowly.

EVERYBODY'S A DAVID

Because I didn't grow up in Sunday school, youth group, Sunday services or midweek prayer meetings, I'm still a novice when it comes to a lot of Christian culture. When I'm around other Christians and they joke about sword drills or roll their eyes at the memory of some song from Christian summer camp, I just try to laugh on cue and then disguise the fact that I'm a beat late by taking a quick sip of my coffee. Until adulthood, the closest I came to church was my Presbyterian nursery school's annual Christmas pageant, in which I served dutifully in the role of sheep number three.

Cradle Christian friends have tried to explain to me the church version of superheroes: the biblical heroes populating Sunday school felt boards. I expect that most of these are from the Old Testament, because unlike heroes in the New, they did stuff that seems fun to kids. Gideon versus Zacchaeus for an audience of five-year-olds? No contest. But you also have to take most of the salt out of a lot of those stories; so kids get David scrapping with Goliath, but not braining him with a rock and then chopping his head off. I suspect that David pulling a Code Red on Uriah, after making the poor Bathsheba a royal offer she had no ability to refuse, gets omitted entirely. Try illustrating that one with a felt cutout.

For adults, the Christian focus on heroes seems to emerge in our tendency to read Bible stories as if they're about us. Imagine you're in a small group at church, and you're reading the story of David and Goliath (the grownup version, not the felt-board version) in 1 Samuel 17. This story is much more complicated than the usual one-line summary. Consider the variety of characters named and their relationship to David, our hero protagonist:

- King Saul sends the hero off to battle;
- Goliath gets killed by the hero;
- Jesse, David's father, underestimates the hero;
- Eliab, David's oldest brother, resents the hero;
- Abner, the Israelite commander, doesn't recognize the hero who saves his army;
- the Israelite army cheers the hero;
- the Philistine army runs away from the hero;
- and, lest we forget, God makes the hero a hero by delivering Goliath into David's hand.

When reading a story in the Bible—or in any book—it's natural to compare yourself to or to identify with one of the characters. As we can see, there are lots to choose from in the story of David and Goliath. But I don't think I've ever seen anyone read it and chuckle ruefully, saying, "Wow, I'm just like Abner, because sometimes God is doing something, and I've got absolutely no idea where it's coming from." I've never heard anyone lament, "Man, I am such an Eliab, because I am always tearing down the person that God's really picked for the job."

No, Christians interpreting this story invariably identify somehow with David. Maybe I'm thinking about how great he is and how I should try harder to be godly like him. Or I'm wondering if there are five attributes, like David's five stones, that I can work on in order to slay my personal giants. Or I realize I haven't talked to so-and-so in a while and that my broken relationship is really the Goliath in my life. Or I think about how I need to take a risk and walk out in faith just like David did when he left behind the armor that was untested and too big for him. Everybody's a David: right at the center of the plot, the hero, the point of the story.

This is funny because most of us are average, historically speaking—and David most definitely is not.

Here's the story in context: God chooses David as king of Israel to replace Saul, who has forfeited his kingship by being unfaithful. David—a singular character in biblical literature, alongside Abraham and Moses in importance in the Old Testament—demonstrates his worth by trusting in God's strength to give the victory, despite Goliath's strength and David's youth. From this launching pad, David goes on to become the defining monarch of Israel, establishing the eternal kingship that will be fulfilled and restored only in the person of Jesus Christ, who is God made flesh.

In other words, the story of David and Goliath marks one of the most significant points in the history of the salvation of the world. The story and event stand alone, incomparable. It is safe to say that not a single moment in any modern reader's life, no matter how understandably significant those moments might seem, plays anything like a similar role in God's salvation history. But for some reason, we neither pause nor blush before leaping in and identifying personally and intimately with one of the most important figures in all of biblical literature—and therefore in human history—to see what life lessons his experience might have for us. "How can I be a hero like David?" we ask.

We can't, is the answer. We're not heroes. We're not historically significant individuals. The vast majority of people reading these words won't be remembered by history. I certainly won't be. If I pause to think about it, I know the names of *some* of my great-grandparents, though little else about them—and they are in my own family. So, when we look at the giants of the Bible, people whose names and deeds are remembered and discussed thousands of years after their deaths, we are looking at people with whom we have almost nothing in common. This is a hard thing to consider, especially in the vigor of youth, but Scripture really is right: we're like the grass of the field, here one day and gone the next. And our passage through life, though it might be incredibly important to those around us, is not particularly significant in any broader context.

Here's where that superhero desire and love for the fight takes Christian form. We all want to save the world. To change it. To make an impact for Jesus. To be a hero. But we are not the center of God's story. We are not God's heroes.

If we want to find ourselves in the story of David and Goliath, we should probably look to verses 51-53; at most, we're the nameless soldiers in the Philistine or Israelite army, watching with either horror or glee as God's inscrutable and unrelenting providence unfolds, and our fates are determined by people and forces beyond our control. We are the biblical bystanders, individuals whose literary analogs are the unnamed people who gather in plurals—crowds, armies, masses—to watch as God's history marches onward.

In fact, if we were to learn one thing from David, it should be what the Israelite armies learned that day, because he told them so before marching out against Goliath: David was great because he knew he wasn't the main character in the story.

THE HEROISM OF FOLLOWING

When superheroes emerged in popular culture in the mid-twentieth century, they were uncomplicated and larger than life. You could tell the good guys from the bad guys by the color of their hats. Since then, however, there's been a gradual trend toward showing heroes' humanity and even their dark sides. It was shocking when now-classic graphic novels like Alan Moore's *V for Vendetta* and *Watchmen* first blurred the line between hero and anti-hero, but this shift now enjoys popular appeal, as demonstrated by films like Christopher Nolan's well-received—and very dark—Batman trilogy.

This deconstruction of the superhero tells us something important about Jesus, and about our callings. After all, the superhero category is, in a fundamental way, unimaginable without Christ. Consider Superman, who looks just like a normal person but is invincible, sent by his celestial father to Earth to save its people. The superhero genre follows a basic pattern of Western literature, in which the narrative crisis is usually some version of the need for redemption, with resolution offered by some form of a savior. In a way, the story of Christ is the only story we know how to tell, whether we believe it or not. We just tell it in thousands upon thousands of ways.

Many of our most beloved characters are stand-ins for Christ—often consciously so. The problem with Christ-figures, as they're called in literary theory, is that they're necessarily incomplete. They can illuminate some aspect of Jesus: from Superman to Aslan to Cool Hand Luke. But each Christ-figure can show us only this or that aspect of Jesus, such as a sacrificial death, a refusal to resist evil, being a healer, a transgressor of boundaries. Each is at best a shadow of the Savior. There is simply no literary figure that can finally stand in for Jesus of Nazareth, Messiah of Israel and Lord of the world.

The inherent limitation of Christ-figures illustrates the dangers of imagining a heroic calling. When we think about saving the world, it is all too easy to focus on one aspect of heroism, like dedication to a cause, ferocity toward evil or willing self-sacrifice. But heroes are only great on paper and in film, where the story can focus on their amazing deeds. Such illustrations of the heroic virtues can and should inspire us. In real life, however, heroes are often distorted figures whose outsized commitment to making something happen carries a cost paid by someone or something else—family, community, conscience and so on. Christians are not free to make such sacrifices. There is nothing God needs us to do so badly that it warrants neglecting some aspect of Christlikeness in our lives. It is in and through Jesus Christ, and him alone, that God has saved and is saving the world.

This is why the stories of heroic Christians throughout history are never stories about what they themselves have accomplished. Instead, they are stories about men and women whose greatness derived from their wholehearted and single-minded devotion to and imitation of the singular hero of history. They are heroes to the degree that they are followers. This heroism is available to every disciple of Christ. And that truth brings freedom and joy.

3

BROKEN BEYOND OUR REPAIR

Getting the World Wrong

The level of sorrow in the world is staggering, and thanks to modern media, we know all about it. It is natural to read the situation as a challenge and ask how it can be fixed. The promise of our progressive, modern age is that the world is subject to repair, given the right willpower and tools. But this assessment fails to account for the shape of the world's brokenness.

First, it overestimates our ability to do good in the present by imagining that our current situation is separate from the past. We cannot escape our connection to history, which is shot through with sin, with evils that cannot be undone. This connection limits the extent to which we can repair the present (or the future) in the same way that it is impossible to paint over a rotten wall or build a large structure on a compromised foundation. We live on top of unmendable cracks, and the insoluble nature of the world means that the question posed to us is not "how do we fix this?" but "how can we live out the love of God the midst of such brokenness?"

Second, the perspective of world saving radically underestimates the nature of the problems we face, especially in the complexity of an era rightly characterized as globalization. The advancement of human capacity means that we increasingly live in a context defined by macro-forces—political, economic, ecological or technological—that simply defy any individual's comprehension or control. But the nature of human experience has not changed apace, which leads us to a confused understanding of the relationship between individual action and systemic change as well as to an inflated view of our capacity to direct the course of human history.

Third, the misdiagnosis of our situation often leads to activist proposals that are radically unable to deliver on their own promises. The challenge to us, then, is how to perceive both the magnitude of the world's brokenness and the smallness of our own capacity, without retreating into paralyzed apathy.

THE ORPHAN

Three decades and a year after I watched the egg explode on the driveway, I lean over a very different ledge—a bridge rail in Hiroshima, Japan, on a hot August night. I am here observing a group of American and Japanese university students on a summer study trip to Japan, and I am about to receive an intimate lesson about how the wounds of history condition the possibilities of our present.

On this day, sixty-six years earlier, the United States had dropped the first atomic bomb on this city. Code-named "Little Boy" and equivalent in explosive force to about thirty million pounds of TNT (fifteen kilotons), the Hiroshima bomb was 1,500 times more powerful than the next-most destructive weapon ever used. This record lasted three days, until the United States dropped another bomb, a twenty-kiloton device called "Fat Man," on the city of Nagasaki. Within four months of the blast, factoring in acute radiation effects, Little Boy and Fat Man had killed approximately 250,000 men, women and children, though the radiation-related death toll continued to rise as years passed.

I stand on the bridge, rendered infinitesimal by the scale of the historical backdrop that surrounds me. From my vantage point, Hiroshima's skyline has faded to invisibility against the night sky, as the day of services remembering and commemorating the bombing draws to a close. The thousands of people who waited patiently in a mile-long line to place a lantern of remembrance in the river have mostly dispersed, and the thinning crowd allows me finally to find space on the bridge to take in the view. As I stare down at the black water ablaze with a snaking rainbow of lanterns, the elderly man to my left—tiny, like so many from that generation of Japanese—glances over and smiles. I smile back.

"Where are you from?" my neighbor asks in cautious, imperfect English.

"The US," I reply.

"Oh!" he says, "that's good! Los Angeles! My cousin lives there."

"I'm from San Diego, California—near LA," I say. We look back at the river, with the comfortable pause of strangers standing side by side.

I glance sideways. "And you? Are you from here? From Hiroshima?" On this bridge, in this city, on this night, we both know that I am asking another unspoken question.

"Yes. From Hiroshima." And then, gently, as if trying to protect me from his words: "My parents were killed by the A-bomb. I was four."

How does one respond to such a thing? In particular, how does a young American, standing on one of the scores of bridges spanning Hiroshima's seven rivers, less than a quarter-mile from the hypocenter of the first atomic bomb ever used in war, dropped by my country on this city, respond to an old Japanese man informing me that precisely sixty-six years and twelve hours ago he was made a four-year-old orphan by a bomb dubbed Little Boy?

If there is protocol or etiquette guiding such a situation, it doesn't

come to mind. So I react naturally, from the gut: first a stunned silence, gazing at the softly smiling face next to me, and then, feeling
the inadequacy of my words: "I'm so sorry."

"It's okay," he says.

But, of course, it's not okay. It's not okay at all.

My words were not, technically, an apology; his were not an abso-
lution. Could they have been? I don't know. On the one hand, we
represented our countries to one another. But on a more profound
level, I lacked the formal stature to make such an offering. I was not
alive when the *Enola Gay* dropped Little Boy over Hiroshima. Even
if I had been, the circle of direct responsibility for using the Bomb
was limited to an even tinier group than the limited number who
knew of its existence. Any of the handful of individuals who could
have *not* made this man an orphan nearly seven decades past, if they
had acted differently, were long dead.

And yet I ached to be able to make an atonement that would offer
peace, somehow make amends for the sorrow of this old man within
arm's reach. I mourned a situation that I could not set right any more
than I could stoop down to lift the earth over my head; I had nowhere to stand. On a collective level, this is the condition and the
tragedy of human history.

My neighbor faced a similar challenge. Even if Harry Truman or
one of the few other Americans who could claim individual moral
responsibility for the atomic bombing were to rise from the dead
and stand before this man, could he grant forgiveness? After all, the
wrong was not his to bear alone. There are thousands of other survivors who still bear in their bodies the sufferings of that day. There
are scores of thousands of stories of loss. And there are hundreds of
thousands of silent dead, like the seventeen thousand whose carbonized, unidentifiable remains rested in a mound a stone's throw
from the bridge where we stood.

Still, his "it's okay" was no perfunctory dismissal of my words. He clearly carried no malice for my country, let alone for me as a person. If he had ever hated America for dropping the bomb that killed his family, that feeling had vanished long ago. In the moment, I failed to recognize the spiritual weight of this fact, but with a bit of distance it astonishes. In the stable comfort of contemporary America, far lesser traumas serve as the foundations for complete personal identities—entire lives orbiting around one sad event. But this man, from whom everything had been taken in an instant, was able to carry it with as little as a small, simple smile.

How could this be? The scope of his loss could never be limited to that one instant of the *pikadon*—Japanese for "flash-roar," the name given to the A-bomb by those first uncomprehending survivors. Instead, the Bomb reached forward in history to shape the architecture of his life: a childhood spent in fosterage, or an orphanage, or one of the gangs of beggar children that roamed post-war Japan; the social stigma that prevented many *hibakusha*, the Japanese term for atomic bomb survivors, from marrying; and the enduring radiation effects that denied some survivors the possibility of bearing healthy children.

Even now, sixty-six years later, the ghost of loss stands next to him in the form of a young American leaning on a balustrade. For if the bomb that made him an orphan had never been dropped, I could have lived my life without having ever heard the word *Hiroshima*, let alone having flown halfway around the world to stand on this bridge—which never would have been built if its predecessor hadn't been destroyed—over the thousands of flaming lanterns that would not have been lit in the hot, humid night to remember those who would not have died in one terrible moment sixty-six years before and in all the terrible moments that followed. As I reflect on his "it's okay," it seems to me that he wanted, not so much to be liberated from the specter of loss, but to liberate it.

He gestures toward the river. "I come here every year to let their souls go free."

On December 7, 1941, the day my grandmother went into labor with my father, this man's nation (if a four-year-old can have a nation) had launched a surprise attack against my country (or, more precisely, the land of my father's and mother's fathers and mothers) at Pearl Harbor. The fact that the Allied nations would later commit sins in their prosecution of the war, culminating at Hiroshima and Nagasaki, should not lead us to false assertions of moral equivalency. It was an era of horrors all around, but the balance scales of judgment tilt decidedly against the Axis powers. The barbarism and cruelty of the Japanese government and Japanese military during the conflict—both toward their Western adversaries and toward other Asians, many of whom still hate them as a result—simply beggars the imagination.

The Japanese seem to recognize this today to varying degrees. Most acknowledge Japanese culpability for the war with the United States. Knowledge of Japanese atrocities committed during World War II is less widespread, as the topic does not receive as extensive a treatment in the contemporary Japanese education system. But the Japanese students I traveled with, who learned this aspect of their history on the trip, exhibited profound shame and remorse over their nation's actions.

Such questions of complicity and agency are one of the greatest and most complex tragedies of war. War is, by definition, waged by nations on behalf of and in the name of its citizens. When wartime is over, the nations make peace—with varying results—and move on. Their governments reestablish relations. They go about their business.

But it is not so easy for their citizens to make peace, to move on. This is because real people, not some abstract nation, bear war's sacrifices; nations are but stories that describe and bestow collective meaning for a people, and stories do not suffer. Some sacrifices are marked by the vacancies of daily life. Families limp along with great holes punched in them: empty spots at dinner tables, beds, pews. Other sacrifices are marked by what is left behind—the shrapnel of hatred and death left in real people's hearts; it is nearly impossible to rehabilitate our image of an enemy who had to be demonized and dehumanized to warrant the war. Governments wage war. But it is people who must live among its wreckage, even decades after the fact.

The lesson came to me in a recognition of the horrors of war. But it was not just about war; it was also about sharing a history that bears the indelible mark of sin. So there we stood, that Hiroshima night, two strangers leaning on a bridge rail over a black, flaming river, neighbors by inches but with a chasm between us that we were powerless to close.

GLOBAL SAMARITANS

Most of us do not have to travel to Hiroshima to know that the world is broken beyond repair. We don't even have to leave Cleveland. Or Birmingham. Or Phoenix. The lives we live are all the evidence we need that there are cracks in the world too shattered to glue back together.

The hard work and best intentions of good and decent people cannot inoculate them from problems that they cannot fix. The fact that so many people share similar stories makes them no easier to bear. The world's brokenness is not out there somewhere, but near to us, in our communities, families, homes and souls. This apprehension sets in quickly when something makes life tumble around us, and as we try to prop it up, we find every handhold crumbling into dust.

Massive suffering is nothing new, but real-time global knowledge of it is. Technology makes the world a small place, broadcasting the cries of need through the shining screens and blaring speakers that fill our days. So we can be simultaneously aware of (at the time of this writing) ongoing devastation in Haiti, radiation poisoning in Fukushima Prefecture in Japan, millions at risk of starvation in the horn of Africa, the atrocities of the Lord's Resistance Army in Uganda, suppression of democracy in Iran, famine and human rights abuses in North Korea, 1.2 million children trafficked for sexual slavery every year around the world—and this is just a the tip of the global suffering iceberg. On top of trying to eke out a decent life for you and your family and to attain a modicum of security, you are exposed daily to a soul-shattering degree of human suffering, unless you take deliberate measures to avoid it.

In this setting, Jesus' command to follow the good Samaritan's example of helping the afflicted can seem like an impossibly tall order. After Jesus finished talking about the Samaritan and after the lawyer got the right answer (we become neighbors by showing mercy to those in need), Jesus told him, "You go, and do likewise."

I want to do likewise. I really, really do. But every time I browse online news, I feel like I'm walking down a fiber-optic Jericho road, and the ditches on each side are filled with billions of people in various forms of distress, all crying out. How can I be a neighbor to all of them? How do I even begin? Even if we accept the validity of "moral proximity"—that we bear special responsibility for those nearest to us—surely the scope of God's love, along with examples from the early church, such as the collection for the Jerusalem congregation, demands some accountability to those far away.

OIKONOMIA: A HOUSEHOLD ORDER

Since the globe-spanning devastation of the Second World War, which united the world in suffering, we have struggled to develop a global economy that can address this need on this scale. By *economy* I don't mean a financial system only. Rather, I'm using the word in the sense of its biblical Greek origin, *oikonomia*. In Greco-Roman society, the oikonomia was the order or plan for the governance of a household, or people under the same roof. The word is a composite of *oikos*, house, and *nomos*, law or custom: house-law. It outlined the hierarchy of family members and servants, the respective duties of household members, the scheme for provisioning the house and so on. In other words, *oikonomia* is the arrangement of a people whose shared identity is based in their shared interest—the welfare of the household in which they all lived. This was considered so important that some households even had a person, called an *oikonomos*, with the job of overseeing all the house's affairs (as in the dishonest manager in Jesus' story in Luke 16).

Oikonomia is used theologically in the New Testament to describe the kingdom of God, perhaps most vividly in Ephesians 1:9-10: God made "known to us the mystery of his will, according to his purpose, which he set forth in Christ as a plan [*oikonomia*] for the fullness of time, to unite all things in him, things in heaven and things on earth" (ESV). So we see that Christ is God's design for arranging his house—that heaven and earth would be united and ordered in him. But our global unity under the kingdom of God—his reign and coming judgment—has always been a matter of theological belief and assertion, rather than visible structure.

The concept of *oikonomia* is also useful in a nontheological sense in that it describes the order pursued by people who share a "roof" in common. In this way, we can speak of national, regional and cultural laws and customs as varieties of overlapping *oikonomia* or economies. Until the mid-twentieth century, there was no global *oikonomia*, because there was no global "house" that required ordering—no global identity based in a universally shared interest. But in our age the speed and immediacy of the connections between us means that an event anywhere on the globe can have immediate effect anywhere else.

To use our house metaphor, there's a big difference between seeing your neighbor's house on fire across the street and worrying it might eventually spread to your own, and seeing your neighbor's house on fire when you live on the other side of a duplex, sharing walls and a roof. In an earlier time, what happened in Zimbabwe was Zimbabwe's business and what happened in Britain was Britain's business (except for colonial interest).

The invention of nuclear weapons changed all that. In a singular way, it transformed the nations of the world from a scattered set of houses into one building, like a row of townhomes. When the American president and Soviet premier oversaw a nuclear system that had the ability to kill every living thing on the planet, nobody could say that we didn't share the same roof—in the nuclear respect, at least. Nuclear weapons were just the beginning—the rafter beam of a new global house that perpetually threatened to come down on all our heads.

At the dawn of the twenty-first century, we are plagued by a host of truly global crises. Some I mention above, such as trafficking. Add to this the globalization of financial markets as well as manufacture and supply chains in which a collapse anywhere can trigger collapse everywhere; the threat of catastrophic pandemic disease in an era of rapid transcontinental travel; climate change, which is already manifesting in many and terrifying ways; looming resource crises around clean water and fossil fuels; and the underregulated progress in nano- and biotechnologies. Some problems are local, national or regional; these aren't. These are major issues that affect everyone on the planet, regardless of citizenship. However, though these problems plague our global house, we have struggled to develop an *oikonomia,* a household order that can address them.

Today's global crises exist because we no longer simply live *in* the world but also *over* it. The conditions of life on the planet are no longer something that just happens to us. We also affect them through the collective behavior that shapes global systems—for example, how we consume resources or whether we engage in nuclear war. But while the problems of our collective behavior are over the whole world, our *oikonomia* cannot get on top of those systems to govern them.

It's important to note that when I say global *oikonomia,* I'm not talking about (nor advocating for) global *government*—a single body to rule the whole world. Instead, I'm referring to global *governance,* which means the structures, whether strong or weak, through which we deal with issues happening on a worldwide scale, bigger than any one nation's ability to deal with.

Moreover, global governance is not a question of some future "whether," but rather a present "how." We are already doing global governance through structures of varying effectiveness that attempt to resolve issues bigger than any one nation's borders—for example, the United Nations, transnational economic associations like the G-8 and G-20, NATO, OPEC and the Organization of American States. But in these very structures we see why a global *oikonomia* (by which I mean *governance*) differs profoundly from national, regional or even household economies: at the global level, there is not—and never can or should be—a singular authority to make decisions and resolve problems.

It might help to imagine a contrast. Say your child's elementary school had a bullying problem caused by a number of factors: an indifferent principal, inadequate teacher supervision, disengaged parents, a student culture of bullying. You could isolate these problems and find ways to exercise authority over them. You could pressure the principal by appealing to the district superintendent and demand a change in teacher supervision structures and schedules that permit the bullying. You could host a parents' meeting to help build commitment in the home against bullying. You could put together a student assembly that would address why bullying is so bad. In sum, it is a problem that you could tackle from above. You could get on top of this situation.

However, other than the reign of God, there is no "above" when it comes to global crises like poverty and nuclear weapons. There is no earthly superintendent to appeal to, and we are all children, even our leaders. We are used to solving problems from the top, because every other problem in life works that way. But these issues are so big, so high up, so global, that we can get at them only from below. If we change the behavior of one group, it won't fix things, because all parties need to change. The issue is not indifference but complexity.

The intrinsic challenge of this situation leads to two profound consequences for would-be Samaritans on the world's Jericho Road. First, *the fact that we are collectively culpable for global crises leads to the overestimation of our individual capacity to be part of a solution.* For example, the clothing I am wearing may not have been produced, shipped and distributed in an ethical manner. As I sit and type these words, I may be wearing the fruits of labor that borders on slavery and contributes to poverty. I hope this isn't the case, but that hope is probably delusional.

Though my individual action is part of the problem, I'd be wrong to think that a change in my behavior would, in itself, be a small part of its solution. In theory I could make my own clothes out of locally made cloth that I know wasn't produced via exploitation or environmentally damaging practices. Then I wouldn't be personally complicit in the problem anymore. But my doing so wouldn't do anything to solve the overall problem of unjust manufacture. Moreover, my support of local harvest and individual manufacture—basically a pre–Industrial Revolution means of production—is simply an inadequate response to the challenge of clothing a world with seven billion people, especially by the standards of the developed world.

Don't get me wrong here. I'm not denying the capacity of collective action to help make changes in corrupt systems, such as the boycott of apartheid-era South Africa that helped undermine that regime. We could transform the problem of unjust manufacture, for example, if we could figure out a way to develop strong practices of justice in a global *oikonomia*—our worldwide household order. That's a tall order, though imaginable. But the key takeaway here is that actions I take as an individual, though meaningful and intrinsically worthwhile on a personal level, are meaningless to the system of injustice *unless* they are channeled strategically through a strategy of collective action. And the challenge of executing such strategies is commensurate to the size of the targeted system. A Facebook campaign won't cut it.

The second consequence is more fundamental: *our realization that we are collectively responsible for the stewardship of the world can lead to the belief that we can fix its brokenness altogether.* When I tell people that I make a living working for the abolition of nuclear weapons, they often respond with a remark about saving the world. Though flippant, such comments betray a hint of the conviction that we could do it, we really could save this thing, if we just got our act together.

Right now we are seeing a generational shift, especially in younger Christian circles, toward engaging problems as complicated systems—for example, looking at poverty in terms of wealth creation and development rather than simple charity. This marks an embrace of a historically progressive perspective, which sees such issues at the collective level: fix the social cause, fix the problem. The

shift is a good one in many respects, because it attempts to recognize
the true complexity of such issues.

But there is an enduring wisdom to the historically conservative
perspective as well, which sees issues at the level of individual choice
and moral agency. The truth of every social ill combines both individual decisions and social factors. Even if every social condition
were perfected (a task that I would argue is impossible), the human
heart would remain catastrophically broken, "deceitful above all
things and beyond cure. Who can understand it?" (Jeremiah 17:9).
The story of our genesis tells us that a perfect people in a perfect
place still failed to choose God; what hope, then, does a humanity
born with congenital spiritual weakness have? Our intrinsic willingness to choose wickedness and selfishness corrupts even the best
systems we can design.

This does not mean that we have permission to run from problems,
even massive ones. The abolition of chattel slavery in the eighteenth
and nineteenth century was an unadulterated good, despite the fact
that such legal developments could never excise our desire to be
lord over our fellow beings and despite the fact that other forms of
slavery persist today. The work of abolishing nuclear weapons is
similar: it is not about curing people of our willingness to kill each
other en masse, but about regulating a technology so that certain
disastrous avenues are closed to us. It *can* be done; whether we will
do it remains to be seen. With examples like these, we cannot regard
the challenge of injustice as an excuse to avoid confronting it. It is
possible to make the world look more like heaven.

But we should not confuse our ability to undertake fundamentally *tactical* efforts—that is, working on highly specific, discrete,
comprehensible problems—with an ability to transform the existential condition that gives rise to injustice in the first place. We are
in trouble if that is the goal that motivates our work. Those who

have aimed at utopia have often been the most effective at unleashing hell on earth.

Our situation and its two consequences—we cannot individually fix problems in which we are complicit, and we must steward and manage a world that we cannot fix—seem to leave us in a terrible bind. We feel a responsibility that we cannot discharge. We all want to save the world, but we can't. So what do we do?

We begin by telling the truth.

SINNER'S PRAYER ACTIVISM

The profound challenge of our context often leads to proposed solutions that are inadequate to the tasks that they take on. A core dilemma for contemporary activists is how to establish an honest correlation between the problems we purport to address and the strategies and tactics we employ in doing so.

A while back, I came across an article that suggested that modes of religious activism tend to mirror the community's particular structure. For example, the article hypothesized that Roman Catholics, who have a large, disciplined and regimented church hierarchy, are naturals at engaging a large, disciplined and regimented hierarchy like the US government.

So I started thinking about the attributes of the evangelical churches I know best. I came up with a list of good things: creative, outside-the-box thinking; a genius for good communication; entrepreneurial spirit; can-do attitude; relentlessness, engagement and passion. All of these emerge out of a zeal to share the gospel as widely and as compellingly as possible. And, in general, I think they accurately correspond to most activist efforts that I'm familiar with.

But if the good parts of the church lead to good parts of activism, we have to be honest about the effect of the bad parts too. When evangelism goes wrong, churches can turn to a shallow conversionism.

It looks like this:

1. You are confronted with a quick pitch describing a huge problem (sin).

2. You are implicated for your personal complicity in the problem, and this complicity has consequences (going to hell).

3. You are presented with a quick and convenient way to absolve yourself of personal responsibility in the problem, which entails zero short-term cost.

This last step is the sinner's prayer, which goes something like this: "Jesus, I'm sorry for my sins, and I want you to come into my heart as my personal Lord and Savior." On one level, such simple repentance is the right response to freely given grace. But in the context of real life, the sinner's prayer barely begins to scratch the surface of a life lived in continual repentance, that requires carrying the cross daily in the accountability and encouragement of Christian community and that entails an exhaustive calling to sanctification and vocation until the day you die. If the sinner's prayer stands alone, it misses the point, giving the pray-er a false sense of what salvation and a life in Christ are truly like.

I call nonprofit work based on the same model "sinner's prayer activism," and I have been both its occasional perpetrator and its victim. Sinner's prayer activism is attractive because it is essentially cost-free, which is appealing to anyone who is already working like crazy to live a decent life but who can't shut out those cries from the global Jericho Road.

THE CAUSE VIDEO

Sinner's prayer activism is epitomized in the variations on a video that's shown at every Christian conference I attend or speak at. No matter the cause, the basic script always goes like this:

Step 1: Set the scene. The feel you are going for is *haunting*.

Dark screen. Ominous, slow percussion. Then cue keening, sad and vaguely Irish-sounding music. Imagine you ran over Enya's dog— yep, that's it.

Step 2: State the Big Problem in a dramatic way.

"Did you know that every day, people worldwide suffer from Big Problem X?"

Step 3: Insert a subject that will induce feelings of charitable sympathy in a mostly white, middle-class audience, followed by a terrible verb, followed by the biggest number you can use without lying outright. Decorate with a sense of urgency and any relevant details.

"In the time it takes to watch this video, vulnerable subject A will suffer/ die by the millions because of Big Problem X. Details, details, details, etc." [Close-up photo of sad child's face. Bonus points for flies.]

Step 4: Now you have reminded your audience that the world is not a nice place. Because they are good and decent people, this reminder makes them sad. The sentimental are weeping and the righteous are angry. Give them hope, fire them up, and bring 'em back.

"Fortunately, a solution is possible." [Sudden upswing in music: cue happy, vaguely African-sounding percussion.]

Step 5: Name a ludicrously simple solution to Big Problem X, and implicate your viewer with a quick switch to first-person plural.

"The average American's annual sock budget is twenty-three dollars. If we stopped wearing socks for just one month, we could SOLVE Big Problem X! But we can't do it without you."

Step 7: Blend up a smoothie of empowering-sounding activist jargon. Dynamic verbs are mandatory; coherence is optional. Your goal is to channel emotion into action.

"The time to take action is now! Stand up! Let your voice be heard! Act out!"

Step 8: Close the deal with an easy action step that is ridiculously disproportionate to Big Problem X.

"Like us on Facebook and follow us on Twitter today, and visit our website to learn more and help raise awareness about Big Problem X."

Step 9: Finish strong.

"Together, we can [optional, for bonus points: *be the generation to] make a difference/impact."*

Fade to website address on black background.

Saving the world has never seemed so easy, has it? Christians eat these videos up—at least, those of us who make the videos think they do.

So we "fast" from some daily indulgence. We wear the rubber bracelet. We text our ten-buck donation to some shortcode. We buy those shoes that give some kid somewhere shoes. We break our indulgence fast but only when it's fair trade. We buy the T-shirt. Of course we do. If there's a combed organic cotton T-shirt with a slick, soy-ink discharge print that will save lives somehow, you're darn right I'm buying it. Sign me up for two.

If I seem to be casting the first stone here, trust that I am heaving it straight into my own eye. I don't mean to be unduly harsh on my fellow activists. Just because an action doesn't fix a wholesale problem doesn't make that action useless. Like the kid saving the starfish in that story I hate,* doing a little good is precisely that: a little good. It matters to the people it matters to, and that in itself is pleasing to God. But there is a categorical difference between trying to make the world a better place and trying to fix it entirely. It is important to shine a light on the ways in which world-fixing impulses are often subtly at play in our activist behavior.

The problem with sinner's prayer activism is that despite the good intentions of its purveyors (having been there and done that, I promise that most of us are really just trying our best) it is a bill of goods, at best a half-truth. It convicts us with unfathomable problems and then invites us into shallow responses. In doing so, it soothes our grief and placates our outrage with actions that are wholly inadequate to either. It comes out of a good place: the recognition that if I'm going to burden people with a concern, I have a pastoral responsibility to help them channel it. But if we're going to talk about the massive crises we talk about, we have to tell the truth. We can neither escape nor solve the fundamental tragedy of life and this world.

Big problems are not easy. There are cost-free ways of making yourself feel better about them, but there aren't cost-free ways to tackle them. When I come to Christ as a repentant sinner, I can receive in faith a spiritual confidence and assurance of my salvation and the love of God. But my reward is still a ways off. In the meantime, I will live as an alien to the world my parents brought me into, having transferred my citizenship to a kingdom that is both invisible and future. I live in faith that it is coming, gaining my strength from that hope, and this shapes my life in the image of love. But I can't expect the road to be easy. In fact, it will be so difficult that it requires a

---

*"'It matters to *this* one!' the child screeched at the stunned man on the beach, before heaving the hapless invertebrate into the raging sea, minus one twitching leg that remained in his hammy little fist. . . . "

community of pilgrims to sustain each other on the way. And though the rewards are abundant, if subtle, I can't expect a full payout on my wager in this lifetime.

ON A DARK BRIDGE OVER A FLAMING RIVER

In response to the litany of human woes filling the pages above, some may be saying, "Okay, okay, I get it—the world is terrible! So, what's the secret? What's the plan? What's the solution?"

There is no secret. No plan. No solution—until the kingdom of God comes—to the dilemma of living in a fallen world. That's the point. The answer is not a course of action, a recipe, a hidden formula. *But the absence of evident solutions does not absolve us from the pain of loving the world as Christ loves it.*

Confronted with this tension, the only response is resolute commitment. We can realize that there is no solution and simultaneously refuse to be defeated or paralyzed by that fact. We can ensure that the solutionlessness of our condition does not harden our souls. We can labor against injustices so vast that their remedy is beyond our capacity to execute and in spite of the knowledge that we are unlikely to see their resolution.

This is no abstract suggestion. A generation of Christians that thinks it is called to save the world is a generation firing on the fuel of false hopes. It is signing up for exhaustion and disillusioned burnout. I can already see its signs in the audiences I speak to and the people I meet. It is imminent. And, for the love of God, we can't afford to let that happen.

The chasm that I discovered between me and my friend on that Hiroshima bridge was the terrible reality of living in a fallen world. The gap between me and the man on the bridge was profound; it was greater—in a real and concrete way—than the gap between me and my neighbor, or me and the person ahead of me in line at the grocer, or (probably) me and you. But it is not fundamentally different.

The sin of the world is not some minor laceration. Our good choices and decent lives cannot salve and stitch it into nothingness. Yes, repentance, forgiveness and reconciliation can turn our individual scars into beauty marks. But our sin as a species is no clean cut. It is a vast and ragged puncture wound driven deep into the lungs and heart of creation itself. The divide stretches between us and God, and between every person and every other person. Even if we cared enough or were good enough to work in perfect concert to try to fix it (though we don't and aren't, and thus we won't), we lack the capacity. The wound of sin is the very ground on which we live, eking out our unpredictable lives along its edges.

Back on the bridge, Kaori—one of our group's translators—comes up to me and the man. I introduce him clumsily: "I was just speaking with this gentleman. His English is much better than my Japanese. He is *hibakusha*. The bomb killed his parents."

They exchange bobbing, rapid bows and begin speaking in Japanese. After a few moments, they pause, and Kaori says, "He wants you to know that he is glad you are here. He is glad that a young American would come to see Hiroshima. He thinks that war is terrible, and he says that the only way to prevent its suffering is to pursue peace. Not just with words, but with deeds. With things we can do together."

He is talking about incarnating a love that lunges to stretch across a brokenness that it cannot repair. This is what fellow travelers who met on a bridge over a flaming darkness and are separated by an unbridgeable gap attempt to do.

We cannot mediate our own divide, we cannot solve the problem of our condition; another has done that for us. But in recognizing that all that is necessary has been offered by grace, we are freed to extend and receive compassion however God gives us ability. We can feel one another's hurts, rejoice in one another's joys. We can have an interest in one another and make the other's welfare our own. And we can do this, not simply with words, but also through the deeds of ordinary people living in this world.

4

FEAR GOD

Getting God Right

Christian activism is grounded in claims about God. It's about how we understand our role in God's will being done "on earth, as it is in heaven." Different theologies give us different pictures of our relationship to the manifest will of God, ranging from the hands-off "let go and let God" approach, to that of human beings as "co-creators" of the kingdom alongside the divine.

The way we understand the relationship between God and our earthly work matters a great deal. After all, in *Christian* activism we can't be pure pragmatists, saying that situation X would be materially better if we employ solution Y. No, we are making assertions about the intention of the Creator of the universe—a rhetorical trump card if ever there was one. So Christian activism does not merely *invoke* the will of God; it is equally a *witness* to it. And telling the truth about God—in biblical parlance, not taking God's name in vain—is a fearful, weighty matter.

Two perils of the activist spirit are that we will get ourselves or the world wrong, as the previous chapters caution against. But it is far worse if our activism offers an incorrect or even false testimony about God. When we are trying to save the world, it is an all-too-ready temptation to search for a God who will validate our pre-existing purposes—a sort of cosmic Fix-it Man. The misrepresentation is seldom willful; I don't know any Christian activists who intentionally misuse God's name willy-nilly. But I think a great many of us frequently speak about God, in relation to our work, in ways that domesticate the divine to our earthly causes.

What does it look like to correct this distortion? We need to remember that God defines, rather than supports, our positions. And this requires coming to terms, as best we can, with who God is and what God's purposes are. The results are profoundly uncomfortable. Not for nothing does the Bible speak of the "fear and trembling" accompanying true faith. This fear of God is precisely what must be recovered for Christian activism to be faithful.

THE GOD ON MY LEASH

The nineteenth-century philosopher Ludwig Feuerbach theorized that we make our own gods by worshiping a projection of ourselves. This, he said, is why god is so powerful. Feuerbach was wrong about God, but right about us. How often and in what ways do we worship a version of God that confirms what we think and validates who we think we are?

The danger for those who care about causes is that God winds up playing the role of the parent—"because I told you so!"—when we get tired of making our case. For example, it's easy to talk about God as a God of justice and peace or as a God who loves families. I happen to think these statements are true. But they're also a good deal more complex than we often allow.

For example, God the lawgiver gave the Israelites ample instructions about how to treat their slaves—but didn't prohibit them from having them in the first place. God brings *shalom*, peace, but God is also a warrior who commands the angelic hosts, killing entire cities and armies in one stroke. Yes, family seems to be the basic unit of created human community, but the rampant polygamy in the Old Testament is not always condemned. Also, Jesus seems fairly clear in his replacement of biological ties with the bonds of faith, as is Paul's Spirit-inspired directive that celibacy is somehow superior to marriage.

Don't get me wrong, I don't believe that Christian ethical teaching permits slavery, loves war or allows polygamy. But don't we often invoke God as if the divine purposes line up perfectly behind the moral sensibilities of our culture? A god I can lead around on a leash isn't much of deity. To fasten that chain around his neck I have to shrink him down to a manageable size. The fundamental dilemma here is that (a) God cannot be leashed, which means (b) that the scrawny little rodent I've got collared to my agenda is not, in fact, God, and worst of all, (c) the *real* Deity is standing right behind me and is not super thrilled with my dancing monkey-god show.

The alternative is the "God of the Bible." But invoking that phrase doesn't end discussion. Usually when people use that term they mean the God *they* think is in the Bible, which of course misses the whole point. None of us has a lock on "the biblical God." Engaging the living God of Scripture is a daunting and always dynamic task, worthy of fear and trembling and most of all humility. God can always show up and prove us wrong, after all.

A couple years after the voice in the stairwell saying, *The world is not yours, not to save or to damn. Only serve the one whose it is,* I still didn't understand this. As a peace activist and a novice Christian, I was still trying to put God in the box that validated the anti-nuclear positions I already held. I'll ruin the ending for you and say that God does, in fact, hate nuclear weapons. But this is a wildly different thing than God supporting *my* anti-nuclearism. Ponder Joshua, who asked the angel standing in front of him if he was for the Israelites or their enemies and got the response, "No, I am the commander of the army of the Lord" (Joshua 5:14, paraphrase). It took me a while to get it.

After I heard the voice of God, I chased this unknown "one whose the world is" into seminary study, where I began reading the Bible. The stories that were old hat to my classmates were new and wonderful to me, with all their shine and sharp edges intact. Though it was a long time ago, I still remember the first time I read the story of Jesus cursing the fig tree (Mark 11:12-14, 20-21): Jesus is hungry, and this fig tree has leaves but no fruit for him to eat, so he curses it, and it dies. I remember that it felt shocking and arbitrary and kind of sad. I was sorry for the fig tree, and I tried to think up ways that the episode might mean something other than exactly what it means. Surely God is too tenderhearted for such an act.

I still knew very little about God.

BEHOLDING THE AMORITE

In Deuteronomy, we see the Israelites on the verge of leaving their forty-year sojourn in the wilderness to occupy the land that God has promised them. Moses, full of the Spirit of God, tells them how to make war (Deuteronomy 20:10-18). When they approach an enemy city, they are first to offer peace. If this is accepted, then the population will become the Israelites' slaves, which turns out to be the best-case scenario. If the peace offer is not accepted, the Israelites are to besiege the city, and when God gives them victory, they are to kill every adult and adolescent male and to take the women, children, livestock and property as God's reward to them.

But even that level of conquest isn't the extreme case. That's reserved for when the city belongs to the people who previously held the land promised to Israel. In that situation, God says, "Do not leave alive anything that breathes. Completely destroy them . . . as the LORD your God has commanded"—so great was the wickedness and danger of these nations' idolatry (Deuteronomy 20:16-17).

That's precisely what the Israelites did. Joshua 6:20 records the trumpeting fall of Jericho's wall. This story is popular in children's Sunday school classes because it involves loud noises and something falling down, which is the Bible equivalent of the fun afforded by making a sandcastle and then running away screeching with joy as a wave demolishes it. But in the following verse, we read that "they devoted the city to the LORD and destroyed with the sword every living thing in it—men and women, young and old, cattle, sheep and donkeys." One wonders how many Sunday school teachers include the fact that the wall's fall led to the divinely ordered slaughter of Jerichoites who were the same age as their pupils.

We are understandably tempted to use the distance of time and the absence of gruesome detail to inoculate ourselves from the true horror of such texts. Sometimes we also disguise them by pointing to other places where God condemns violence—like King David being forbidden from building the temple because he was a "man of blood." Such strategies also enable more eschatological interpretations, which see episodes like the Canaanite extermination in the big context of salvation history. This is a legitimate interpretative strategy because Christians have to see all reality through the lens of the cross, resurrection and coming kingdom.

But when we use such approaches exclusively, we lose something profound and powerful: the way in which Scripture challenges our preexisting view of God and of his purposes. Consider the Israelites' confrontation with the Amorites, recounted in Deuteronomy 2:32-36:

When Sihon [the Amorite, king of Heshbon] and all his army
came out to meet us in battle at Jahaz, the LORD our God delivered him over to us and we struck him down, together with
his sons and his whole army. At that time we took all his towns
and completely destroyed [Hebrew: "dedicated to the LORD"]
them—men, women, and children. We left no survivors. But
the livestock and the plunder from the towns we had captured
we carried off for ourselves. . . . Not one town was too strong
for us. The LORD our God gave us all of them.

Eschew every theological escape hatch and confront the text in
its granular historicity. What this passage describes, hidden in the
plain sight of its spare prose, is an Amorite woman, baby in arms,
watching in terrified grief and unredeemable despair as an Israelite
soldier, acting on the commandment of God, kills her entire family
before ending her life as well. The fact that this episode is part of a
history that will directly lead to Christ's giving himself for the world
on the cross is certainly no comfort to her as she watches her children
being slaughtered.

This is not fiction. The Amorite woman is no literary device but a
human being with a name—though it is lost to history. When I
imagine her face, I cannot functionalize her loss and sorrow. If I ever
imagined God as the ribbon tied around a neatly wrapped moral
universe that corresponds perfectly to my twenty-first-century sensibilities, her gaze rips that vision to shreds.

There it is, in its starkest terms. The Bible testifies that God—
whom Jesus Christ calls *Abba*, Father—is a God whose purposes in
history have been served by the killing of children. God has both
commanded it (for example, Deuteronomy 20:16) and wrought it
directly (for example, Exodus 11:4-5). This fact cannot be avoided or
apologized away. What do we do with this?

Such passages close off any possibility of imagining that God's purposes and ways are immediately benevolent to our own, as we understand them. Let's be honest about how we encounter the story above: no modern Christian, transported back in time and space to stand and watch an Israelite army kill every living thing in an Amorite town, would open his *Life Application Study Bible for Teens,* tap an approving finger on Deuteronomy 20 and take God's side. Everything in us sides with the mother and children being killed. We have no choice in this, and we aren't wrong in feeling this way. I certainly wouldn't want to meet someone who could walk away from the scene dry-eyed.

But—and here's the hard part—neither may we judge God to be wrong. From what moral ground would we render such a verdict?

The teaching value of such Scriptures, therefore, is not that they give us a normative ethic about how to make war. Rather, they instruct us by leaving us in a tension before God that does not permit cognitive resolution or rationalization. Faced with such Scriptures, we can pick one of four options:

1. hate God;

2. become monsters—for example, by concluding that the holy wars of ancient Israel permit contemporary crusade or genocide;

3. deny that God is really like this;

4. fear God.

The first two choices are idolatry—either judging God by our standards or elevating ourselves to his. The third denies the scriptural portrait of God that Jesus himself taught and affirmed—and if you toss out the God of the Old Testament, Jesus is the Messiah, Savior and Son of nothing. Which leaves us with the fourth.

I cannot see a way out of this tension. It must be inhabited. It is the ground of our spiritual journey, and it makes the biblical idiom of "fear and trembling" very, very real. It is the recognition that the goodness of God is so alien in its holiness that human life must encounter it in awestruck fear and perhaps something resembling terror and horror. We are left with a God who in no way may be domesticated to serve any earthly project.

"The LORD gave, and the LORD has taken away; blessed be the name of the LORD" (Job 1:21 NRSV). This is a true statement, but for human beings it also bears the inescapable quality of tragedy. If we can say it and mean it without tears, we haven't been paying attention.

THE NAKAZAWAS AND THE TAODAS

Seeking after God has transformed my anti-nuclear work. I used to think about the horror of nuclear weapons as fundamentally *quantitative*—that is, these bombs, even more than other bombs, kill lots and lots of people. So these bombs were dropped, and this many people died, and the badness of the act is measured in the number of digits in the death count.

What I have discovered in seeking the God who saves the world is that the horror of nuclear weapons—for they are horrible—is *qualitative*. The wickedness of Hiroshima and Nagasaki is not that hundreds of thousands of people died, but that innocents were killed—period. The number of innocents simply illustrates and magnifies the transgression. This is the inherent offense of nuclear weapons: as weapons of indiscriminate death, whose unique capacity is to destroy entire cities in a single action, they trespass against the God who made human beings in his image and who holds life and death in his hands.

So consider Hiroshima from close up, instead of our usual vantage point, which is big enough to frame miles-high mushroom clouds and six-figure casualty statistics. Consider it intimately—from the perspective of the trespass—and you will find that it becomes a story about God.

There is a little boy named Keiji Nakazawa standing in front of the gate of his elementary school in Hiroshima on a hot August morning in 1945, speaking with a friend's mother. Then there is a blinding light and deafening roar, and he is knocked unconscious. When he wakes up, he sees his friend's mother's charred body and realized that he has been protected from the heat blast by the school wall. Dazed, he makes his way home and discovers a smoking ruin. He continues to wander the city. Later in the day, he finds his mother, who holds an hours-old infant girl—his sister.

What had happened was this: When the bomb exploded, his mother, in her third trimester of pregnancy, was at home with his father, sister and brother. Then there was a flash and a roar, and the house collapsed.

When his mother dug herself out of the rubble, she saw a carbonized human shape where her daughter had been sitting. She heard the voice of her son, crying out under a pile of roof timbers. She heard her husband from under another pile, asking, "Can't you do something for him? Can't you do something for him?" These three things barraged her stunned brain through her eyes and ears: her daughter's burnt corpse, her son crying out, her husband pleading.

She tried to pull the wreckage away to free her son, but her hands were burned, and she lacked the strength. Then she saw that houses nearby were on fire and that the blaze was approaching their house. A neighbor passed by, and she begged his help.

But he replied, "No, we must go! We must go, for the fire is coming!"

"No!" she said. "I will stay and die with my family." But for her sake he forced her to leave. "No, no, no!" As she was pulled away from her home, she heard, over the roar of the fire, the sounds of her husband and son being burned to death under the roof timbers.

The shock drove her into early labor, and hours later she gave birth to a baby girl. The baby died two months later from radiation sickness and malnutrition.

After her husband, two daughters and son had been killed, Mrs. Nakazawa lived another two decades. She cared for and educated her remaining son, Keiji. He became a famous author of *manga*, Japanese comic art, and wrote the *Barefoot Gen* series based on his experiences.

I heard the story of Keiji Nakazawa's family from his own mouth. He told it in hallmark *hibakusha* fashion, without a hint of self-pity or sentimentality—and perhaps understandably so: what verbal affect could add to the bare truth? But our translator, a mother of young children, wept and wept and wept with the cruel labor of making his words her own.

Or let us go even closer, to a point so intimate it is obscene. While walking in Hiroshima's A-bomb museum, I encounter a Plexiglas case containing a tiny pair of linen shorts, mottled tan and brown and rust-red, and a photograph of a laughing, impossibly chubby little boy. The exhibit card labels it as "Son's underpants."

It tells the story of Ren Taoda, a thirty-year-old mother carrying her two-year-old son, Hiroo, when the bomb exploded. She was terribly burned, except for the Hiroo-shaped patch on her back where her son absorbed the blast, likely saving her life. They fled. Hiroo, scorched, was desperate for water, but Ren had heard that drinking water would kill him. (The sudden shock of cold water killed many people in Hiroshima desperately trying to soothe their burns, and a rumor rapidly spread that this bomb had made water fatal.) The exhibit card said that, for the sake of her son, "Ren hardened her heart and didn't give him any." He died hours later.

And here, right before me, are the underpants in which he died, stained with the blood and ichor that dripped from his terribly burned body, and which were saved by a mother left with nothing but guilt and remorse. I stand there, transfixed, thinking of my three small nephews.

Son's underpants. I stare at the bloody folds and recognize, like a dog with its nose shoved into its own sick, what we have offered up to our Master.

LIFE BELONGS TO GOD

The moral of this story is not about right or wrong, but about *rights*— to human life, and who has them. The terrible passages of Scripture teach us that human life belongs wholly and only to God, full stop. And none of it—not a cellular micrometer or temporal millisecond— is ours to take.

This does not mean that humans can never kill. The Bible is re- plete with instances of divinely sanctioned life-taking—in the the- ocracy of the Old Testament, for offenses against the covenant and in the political proto-theology of the New (for example, Romans 13:1-7), for human government's rightful restraint of wickedness. The history of Christian theology is also profoundly concerned with how to love one's neighbor in the face of violent threat, which can lead to justifications for killing (for example, the just war tradition).

The common thread in each of these is that no human ever *pos-sesses* the authority to take life. We may be delegated that authority on a situational and temporary basis. Because all life belongs to God, those who take it must always be acting as God's proxy, for God's purposes—whether in the holy wars of the ancient Israelites, to ad- vance God's salvation history, or in human government, as the min- isters of God's wrath against injustice. You can see why this is a weighty responsibility: to get it wrong is, literally, murder.

To kill outside the boundaries of God's justice is to take from God, in a way, the time and place of a person's death. For this reason, there can be no quarter and no compromise between Christians and pragmatists on the ethics of life and death. In World War II, commanders justified the bombings of civilian centers like Hiroshima and Nagasaki—that is, taking lives that they had absolutely no right to take—with the claim that doing so would save lives in the end. The theological error here is assuming that God's primary concern is numbers, as if God met with the generals at the start of the war and said, "Here's the balance sheet of everyone living. Get this back to me, and keep the bottom line as high as you can, would you?"

At stake is the God-given, inviolable right to human life. This is not to deny that questions of quantity matter. It means something that nuclear weapons kill on an unimaginable scale. But the degree of destruction simply serves to magnify the *categorical* transgression: that we have trespassed against God to "save" a thing that wasn't ours in the first place. This is the lie of the devil, who has, since Eden, told humanity that life and death are ours to adjudicate. We know Scripture's answer to the proposal that we do evil so that good may come: "May it never be!" (Romans 3:4 NASB).

Only in the recognition of God's complete right over all the world—salvation and damnation, life and death, blessing and disaster, joy and suffering—can we understand our utter lack of authority over life. The commandment against murder—which is to say, *any* act of taking human life outside the judgment and justice of God—is absolute.

The working of God is often terrible. But God may be terrible because he is holy, and holiness is fearsome to behold. So, what do we name it when we, who are so deeply profane, arrogate to ourselves the right to ape God, to plant our unholy feet in his sacred place and wreak terror and horror? This is abomination—because the world is not ours.

LOVING THE SUPERNOVA

Christian faith has given me the perception that I exist in God's own time, not my own. It means the standard by which I measure my life has been transformed from the *efficacy* of what I might accomplish to *fidelity* to the only one whose accomplishment truly mattered.

This has not been easy. It challenges, for one: I have moved through enough spiritual peaks and valleys to recognize that the way is hilly, with attendant highs and lows.

Even more, I have been called to a God—*El Elyon,* God Most High—whose living holiness does not easily fit in polite company or in my North American, middle-class morality. The deity of a dead and unthreatening civil religion capable of reducing theology to ethics would be a far more attractive conversation partner. But I have not heard the voice of that god. The voice that I did hear has led me in a surprisingly direct fashion to the God known by the author of the letter to the Hebrews: "It is a fearful thing to fall into the hands of the living God . . . for indeed our God is a consuming fire" (Hebrews 10:31; 12:29 NRSV).

If I did not perceive him through mortality's "glass, darkly," it would mean immolation. A consuming fire—a supernova, more like! Yet there was also that voice in a concrete stairwell. How does the supernova speak so softly or a voice burn so fiercely? If I seek to serve a God whose purposes are so far beyond mine, but which encompass mine in my own salvation, what does the shape of my service look like? If I cannot save the world, what can I do in it?

How positively unbelievable, then—how astonishingly incomprehensible—that in the man Jesus of Nazareth, the supernova heart meets us as love. And in him we find the character of service in a world that is not ours to save.

5

TAKE THESE SNAKES

If Only . . .

The desire to save the world is perhaps nowhere so enshrined as in the basic conviction that everything could be made right if we could just stop bad people from doing bad things. This paradigm is nearly unavoidable in the practice of activism, which is about transforming what we understand as the problem situation into something more desirable. If only everyone would give up their nuclear weapons. If only corporations would act morally. If only same-sex marriage were il/legal. If only everyone realized the dangers of climate change. If only abortion were outlawed. If only everyone would go vegetarian. If only the human traffickers would stop.

In other words, if only that problem *out there* could be dealt with. But this fails to recognize the degree to which we are ourselves the world's most intractable problem. We are not all equally culpable for all wrongs, of course. But the solution to humanity's condition cannot be viewed as the eradication of wrongs and wrongdoers, because we are all implicated. Concrete examples of this truth abound in life, in ways both large and small. But it is perhaps nowhere more evidently displayed than in what is arguably the most challenging political conflict in the world: Israel-Palestine.

WAR PROFITEERING

"There is no one for us to negotiate with," the senior Palestinian representative tells us as we sit around a gleaming conference table on the fourth floor of the headquarters of the Negotiations Affairs Department of the Palestine Liberation Organization.

My day has taken on a touch of the surreal. This morning I woke to a glorious sunrise over the Sea of Galilee, with Capernaum faintly visible in the distance—the hometown of the apostle Peter and the place where Jesus moved after the arrest of John the Baptist and first preached the message to "repent, for the kingdom of heaven is near" (Matthew 4:12-17). Thirty minutes ago, after a whirlwind, day-long tour of the West Bank, our bus whipped around a corner in Ramallah, the de facto Palestinian capital in the Israeli-occupied territories, and pulled up in front of an imposing concrete building. Now I am listening to a top-ranking Palestinian official. Photos of Yasser Arafat and the current president of the Palestinian National Authority, Mahmoud Abbas, hang on the wall behind me. I hope that I am not making an unintended political endorsement simply by sitting here.

Our group of young American Christian leaders and communicators—all broadly evangelical, theologically conservative and politically centrist or center-right—is on a "living stones" tour of Israel-Palestine. This means that in addition to seeing the "dead stones" of traditional pilgrimage sites, we are in the Holy Land to meet with indigenous Christian leaders there, whose communities have followed Christ for two thousand years without moving a single step from the land where Jesus was born, lived, was crucified and was resurrected.

The depth of these people's faithfulness humbles me. For example, the surname of one Lebanese brother that I met means "pastor" in Aramaic, the language Jesus spoke, meaning that the family name comes from the role that one of his forefathers played in leading the earliest churches. The name by which these Christians' Muslim and Jewish neighbors know them—*al-Nasira* and *Notzri*, respectively— also illustrates their lineage: both mean "Nazarene."

But our trip was not only to uncover an ancient past. Meeting these brothers and sisters in the faith means encountering their living history as well. Because these Christian communities are ethnically Arab, their current experience cannot be understood outside the all-consuming, on-the-ground reality of the Israeli-Palestinian conflict. Though Western media reports tend to reinforce the idea that it is a religious conflict between Muslims on one side and Christians and Jews on the other, our eyewitness experience readily shatters that worldview.

Despite making up barely 1 percent of the population of the Palestinian areas of the West Bank and Gaza Strip, the Arab ethnicity that most Palestinian Christians share with their Muslim neighbors puts them squarely on the wrong side of Israeli law. Our delegation's effort to understand their situation has led us here, to the headquarters of the Palestinian authority responsible for governing our brethren. Here a sincere and sincerely frustrated Muslim Palestinian diplomat is venting anger about his belief that the current Israeli government has no real interest in the historic two-state solution of creating a viable homeland for the Palestinians. He spoke as a man at war with himself: at once resolutely committed to peace, but exhausted by the violence that has surrounded his people for so long and backed into a corner without an apparent exit.

But he was not alone in his frustration. Two days earlier, our group had met with a comparable figure on the Israeli side, a high-ranking member of the Knesset, the Israeli parliament, representing the majority party. "We want peace," he exclaimed, over breakfast and coffee, "but there's nobody for us to negotiate with!" He cited his concerns that the Palestinian street did not support the leadership of President Abbas, as well as divisions between Abbas's ruling Fatah party and the more militant Hamas party. As a consequence, he said, there was no way for the peace-loving Israeli government to reach an agreement that would work.

This caused him evident pain. He knew intimately the promise that Israel continues to represent for the Jewish people, having escaped extraordinary religious and ethnic persecution in the land of his birth through a daring rescue operation by the Israeli military. And he believed that Israel's continued existence depended on its ability to negotiate a solution. He was a sincere and serious man.

I asked him whether he thought current Israeli policies, which increasingly limit the rights, territory and movement of Palestinians, would not further radicalize the populace, thus preventing the rise to power of the very type of moderate leader that the Israelis needed for a negotiating partner. He agreed—an admission that spoke to the seemingly unresolvable nature of the conflict, absent some unexpected, game-changing development or alien intervention.

TWO VICTIMS

With no apparent way out, the lure to join one side or the other is strong. Each has a compelling historic grievance. In the immediate aftermath of World War II, Zionist troops displaced 700,000 Palestinian Muslims and Christians (both are ethnically Arab), from their homes between the Jordan River and the Mediterranean Sea. Over the following years, Israeli forces destroyed five hundred Palestinian villages. This war, which culminated in the declaration of the state of Israel, has yielded the world's largest ongoing refugee situation, with two million Palestinian refugees in Israel, the West Bank and Gaza, and another three million in neighboring countries.

Among those Palestinians who stayed, some became Israeli citizens and others came under Israeli control in the 1967 Six-Day War. These communities face brazen injustices and second-class status, both from the Israeli government and from neighboring Arab countries that have been happy to use Palestinian suffering to justify hostility toward Israel, without demonstrating commensurate zeal for alleviating the dreadful conditions of refugees who are fellow Arabs. These injustices are perhaps most evident in the massive separation wall that divides Palestinian territory and in a constant campaign of territorial attrition via Israeli settlements on Palestinian land, which are condemned as illegal by nearly every nation on earth, including the United States.

In the course of our travels, we were eyewitnesses to what seemed a sustained attack on the Palestinian economic and family structure by the Israeli military, through the demolition of homes, refusal to allow new construction and sequestration of ancestral fields and water sources. I saw this firsthand during a visit to the West Bank village of Nabi Salih, where Israeli soldiers have been documented invading Palestinian homes in the middle of the night and photographing the children in a campaign of intimidation. One fourteen-year-old boy had been seized and held by the Israeli military for three days with no access to his parents. He was tricked into signing confessions written in Hebrew, which he cannot read, detailing fabricated terrorist charges against his own family.

The Nabi Salih community, which engages in protest every Friday to dispute the annexation of their community spring by a nearby settlement, is routinely barraged with tear gas. Such breathtakingly systematic violations of Palestinian human rights—alongside less dramatic but more routine injustices around freedom of movement and commerce—cannot fail to leave Christians unmoved—especially given our Christian solidarity with Palestinian brothers and sisters in the Lord.

But the Israeli story also compels our regard. Jews faced centuries of persecution in Christian Europe, during which lethal episodes like the Spanish Inquisition and the pogroms routinely punctuated a life of persistent second-class status. The Zionist movement for an independent Jewish homeland began in the nineteenth century as a way to escape Christian persecution of Jews. Zionism took on a special resonance after World War II, in which European Jews suffered the single greatest attempt at ethnic extermination in human history, losing six million persons made in the image of God to the diabolism of the Third Reich.

The historical record therefore validates Jewish fears about existential threats to their people. These fears are further enflamed by the justified perception that they are a minority nation surrounded by hostile adversaries and state-sponsored terrorist groups, who are willing to use tactics like suicide bombings of civilian centers. Residents of Israel live under a threat of violence that most Westerners would and should find intolerable. For example, in the twenty-one months between September 2000 and July 2002, an Amnesty International report documented 130 attacks on civilians—an average of more than one per week. Chanah Rogan, the oldest victim, was ninety when a bomb killed her; the youngest was a baby of five months—Yehuda Shoham—killed by a rock thrown through the window of his family's car.[1]

Compounding the sin of Christian persecution of Jews over the centuries, Christians failed their moral obligation to the Jewish people in the twentieth century in two wholesale ways: many were actively involved in the execution of the Holocaust, and the rest—excluding a lamentably small group of exceptional cases—failed to take any action to prevent or mitigate it. This failure shames the name of our faith and leaves all Christians with a special ethical burden, both to ensure zero tolerance for anti-Semitism and to work for Jewish security and safety. In practice, this means the moral obligation of Christian support for the security of Israel. No historically nuanced critique of Zionism undoes the fact that millions of Jews now make Israel their home, and their safety matters.

Resolution between the two sides seems far off. Many Israelis and Palestinians define allegiance by the zero-sum standard of "if you are not with us, you are against us," forcing a decision in one direction or the other. Unfortunately, American Christians are often happy to oblige. Christian Zionists offer carte blanche support for any action taken by the Israeli government, no matter how shortsighted or unjust. A softer version of this position is mainstream among other political conservatives.* On the other side, some left-leaning Christian groups have often responded to Palestinian suffering by blurring the lines between an opposition to unjust actions by Israel and an opposition to Israel itself, reinforcing the Israeli sensibility that it is alone in the world to achieve its own security.

Israelis and Palestinians each inflict injustice on one another, but we need not pretend that there is parity in their capacity to do so: Israel towers over Palestine in money, military might and foreign support. Over time, however, the higher Palestinian birth rate affords them a demographic advantage.

By defining victory for either side as defeat for the other, the existing terms of the conflict lead mercilessly and irrevocably

---

*Christian Zionism understands the formation of modern Israel as a sign of the impending second coming of Christ. It believes that the modern state of Israel has inherited God's covenant with the ancient Israelites, granting them a divine mandate to the land between the Jordan River and the Mediterranean (and, in some interpretations, the vast majority of the Middle East). Advocates also interpret God's promise to Abraham—that those who bless him will be blessed, and those who curse him will be cursed—as a blanket imperative to endorse whatever the state of Israel does.

toward the ruin of both. This is why Robi Damelin, an Israeli activist who lost her son, David, to a Palestinian sniper, told our group that if we had come to Israel to support one side or the other, we should please just go home. Instead, she pleaded, support Israel *and* Palestine *and* peace. To choose one side over the other is to invest ourselves in the perpetuation of the conflict, rather than its resolution, and this choice will eventually bring disaster down on our ostensible allies.

Such side taking is a very human thing to do. It allows us to pretend that the problem is the other and to avoid facing the truth dwelling somewhere near the heart of every conflict: that under every balance of injustice, humanity itself is the problem. And this is the reason that so few of us, despite our words to the contrary, actually want to save the world. We usually just want our side, whatever it may be, to win.

STARING OUR PROBLEM IN THE FACE

The most incisive biblical exploration of humanity's side-taking problem is hidden in plain sight in the most recognizable verse in the Bible. Virtually everyone, whether Christian or not, knows John 3:16. Its ubiquity on signs at sporting events ensures that "the gospel in miniature," as the verse has been dubbed, is regularly broadcast to millions. The lyricism of the King James Version comes readily to many lips: "For God so loved the world, that he gave his only begotten Son, that whosoever believeth in him should not perish, but have everlasting life."

However, if ever there were an argument for reading biblical texts in their original language, John 3:16 would be it. John 3:16 does not mean what most people think it means, and as a consequence of being the most universally known biblical passage, it may also be the most chronically misinterpreted.

The problem comes with the ambiguity of *so*, as in "God *so* loved the world." In English, *so* reads most easily as a description of *magnitude*—that is, as an answer to the question "how *much* did God love the world?" This isn't exactly wrong, but it's not precisely right either, and a number of versions do us no favors by deciding on this interpretation for us—for example, the New Living Translation reads, "for God loved the world so much that . . . "

A more accurate reading of the Greek word usually translated as *so* is conveyed by more obscure versions like the God's Word Translation: "For God loved the world this way . . ." That is, the point of John 3:16 is not to tell us how much God loved the world, but *how* God demonstrates that love. The degree of love may be implied by the manner—a love demonstrated by offering one's only son must be a great love indeed—but the amount of God's love is not the main point. The character of that love is.

So, what's the significance of this theological nuance? It has to be understood in light of the previous fifteen verses, which detail Jesus' conversation with the Pharisee leader, Nicodemus. Evidently, Nicodemus has been convinced by the transformation of water into wine and has come to Jesus in secret to figure out what's going on. Unfortunately, Nicodemus completely fails to understand anything Jesus is talking about.

Finally, Jesus tells Nicodemus the problem:

> I have spoken to you of earthly things and you do not believe; how then will you believe if I speak of heavenly things? No one has ever gone into heaven except the one who came from heaven—the Son of Man. Just as Moses lifted up the snake in the desert, so the Son of Man must be lifted up, that everyone who believes in him may have eternal life. For God so loved the world . . . (John 3:12-16)

A paraphrase might read like this: "Just as Moses lifted up the snake in the desert, so the Son of Man must be lifted up, so that everyone who believes in him may have eternal life. That's how God loved the world—by giving his only son to be believed in, for the sake of that eternal life."

Here's where it gets interesting, because Jesus is saying that he, the Son of Man, has to be understood like the snake that Moses lifted up in the desert. What snake is this? We turn way back in our Bibles to the book of Numbers, in which the Israelites, having escaped from Egypt, are wandering in the wilderness on their way to the Promised Land.

In brief, this odd little tale goes like this: the Israelites are complaining as usual, in this case questioning God's ability to keep them alive in the wilderness and whining about the quality of their food. God's response to them is to send poisonous snakes into the camp, which bite people, who die. This elicits the desired response: the Israelites stop complaining and go to their long-suffering leader, Moses, asking him to pray that God will take the snakes away. Moses does this, and then the story gets really strange, because God doesn't seem to answer Moses's prayer. He leaves the snakes happily chomping down on the Israelites. However, he does provide an antidote, telling Moses, "Make a snake and put it up on a pole; anyone who is bitten can look at it and live." So Moses makes a bronze snake, puts it high up on a pole, and after that it works like a sort of visual serum, curing any snake-bitten Israelite who looks at it (Numbers 21:4-9).

In the Old Testament, that's pretty much the end of the snake episode. But in Jesus' interpretation of the story, the anomalies of Numbers 21 tell us two key things about the human condition: (1) the nature of our problem, and (2) what it means for God to love us in the midst of this problem.

Consider, first, the nature of the problem. In response to the Israelites' snake problem, God sends them a bronze snake as a cure. That is, the problem and the solution have the same image. Now read this in light of the John 3 passage. Jesus, the Son of Man, is like the bronze snake, but he is a human being. And if the bronze snake shared the image of the poisonous snake problem that it solved, then Jesus' humanity tells us that the problem he cures is humanity. Us. We are our own worst problem.

Humankind, ever complaining, ever hardhearted against God, is sin-bitten unto death. Like the Israelites, we rebelled against God, and like them, we are perishing under the consequences. But God sent the Son of Man, the very image of what plagues us, that whoever believes may have eternal life.

Second, we start to see what it means to say that God "so loved the world"—that is, loved the world in this way—by sending his son. The ancient Israelites prayed that God would take away the snakes that they had brought on themselves. But in Jesus' likeness to the bronze serpent, we see that we are the snakes. So, when we pray to God to take away that which ails us, what we are unwittingly praying for is that God would get rid of *us*.

We are the problem that we beg God to do away with. Quick divine relief from the sorrows and pain of the human condition, the consequences of sin, would simply be annihilation. That is precisely what we would get if God did not "so love the world." It can only be love that God answers our prayer in a roundabout way— not by destroying humanity, but by sending the Son of Man as a cure for our condition.

In this man, Jesus, we see a possibility that our imaginations never could have invented: healing from the ruthless, self-inflicted consequence of our own sin and escape from the false trap of choosing sides in a battle that cannot be won, no matter how hard we fight.

Those who see him lifted high show the rest of us a way out, even from our most intractable conflicts.

So we arrive at the problem with side taking, as in the modern Israeli-Palestinian conflict. A zero-sum conception of the conflict is a false understanding of the issue at hand, namely, that the problem is the other guys—those snakes that plague us. This is not to say that the other side—for both sides—doesn't present its challenges. It is not to say that everyone is good or that all sides in all conflicts are morally equivalent. Rather, John 3:16 simply instructs us that God is not finally on any of our sides, no matter how righteous the cause, because our enmity to him makes all of us simultaneously rebellious Israelites and biting snakes. This changes the way we approach earthly enmity.

WE REFUSE TO BE ENEMIES

Refusing to be your enemy's enemy is no mean feat, but I've seen it done on a hilltop west of Bethlehem, a short drive from the birthplace of Jesus. There, on Palestinian land, a man named Daoud Nassar and his family live on a hundred-acre farm called the Tent of Nations. Their family has tilled the land for generations, yielding olives, grapes and wheat. The hill is ringed by four other hills, on which perch the brand-new buildings of Israeli settlements. The Tent of Nations is extraordinarily valuable real estate, both financially and politically, as the last remaining Palestinian-owned hilltop in West Bethlehem. Israel wants it badly.

The formation of the modern state of Israel in 1948 generated many land disputes, and Israeli law required documentary proof of ownership dating back to the Ottoman Empire, which collapsed in 1917. Though Palestinian families had lived in their homes and villages for hundreds of years, most did not have such documents, and so the Israeli government has been able to seize vast swaths of

Palestinian-owned land and then lease or resell it to Israelis. But Daoud's grandfather, Daher, bought the hill that would become the Tent of Nations in 1916, one year prior to the Ottoman Empire's end, and the family has the papers to prove it.

This has not stopped the Israeli military from attempting to confiscate the land. The Nassars have carried out a two-decade-long court battle to demonstrate the veracity of their claim, racking up expenses of 150,000 dollars. Twice neighboring Israeli settlements have attempted to begin illegal road construction on the farm—a sort of annexation-by-asphalt—which were halted only after the family quickly sought a court order. Once Daoud received a phone call offering him a blank check and official relocation in exchange for selling the land. He refused, because the family land is priceless to him.

Now, with no legal recourse to the land, the government appears to have shifted tactics and decided simply to make life on the farm as unpleasant as possible. Citing "security," they have moved rocks over the road leading to the farm, forcing visitors to park at a distance and walk. The Nassars are not permitted a connection to running water or the electric power grid, though the neighboring Israeli settlements enjoy swimming pools. No buildings are allowed on the property, and standing demolition orders exist for every other structure, including the chicken coop and a Volkswagen van converted into a storage shed. Daoud and his family thus live as their ancestors did, in tents and in the surprisingly homey lime-washed caves that dot the land. And though removed from the property itself, the Israeli West Bank barrier—a twenty-six-foot-high concrete wall planned to snake 470 miles through Palestinian territory—threatens the farm with almost total isolation from the outside world.

Threats of overt violence pepper the ambient hostility. On one occasion, the Nassars were driving late at night from the farm to Bethlehem to attend worship services the following morning.

Without warning, a group of Israeli soldiers burst out of the undergrowth to either side of the road, their faces painted and their weapons ready. After stopping the car, they ordered Daoud to wake and remove his young children, sleeping in the back seat, so that they could inspect the vehicle. On another occasion, soldiers arrived at the entry to the farm and beat down the gate. The nearby settlers have uprooted hundreds of olive trees, and harm to the family and their guests hangs constantly over the farm—the settlers are armed, aggressive and given a legal presumption of self-defense in any conflict.

In sum, the farm seems to refine the Israeli-Palestinian conflict down to its purest distillate: a battle waged over land, along a combat front of ethnicity, employing the weapons of law, intimidation, sequestration and terror, with banners of fear and humiliation marking the opposing sides. Taken in the abstract, the Tent of Nations makes side taking a tempting option. When I visited and heard the stories of the place, I readily imagined how I might react to being subjected to such injustice; to having to bear its financial expense; to being denied basic utilities like housing, water and power; to the constant threat of violence against me and my family; to fixing a gate that others destroyed for no reason; to being forced to wake sleeping children and pull them from a car, terrified, into the midst of a squadron of foreign soldiers with painted faces and enormous automatic weapons. In considering these scenarios, my anger overcame the best intentions of my theology.

"Pray that the Lord will take the snakes away from us," indeed—and if there were ever a situation where a man might be expected to pick up a gun, this would be it.

But listen to the miracle of God's sovereign grace: on the last Palestinian hill in western Bethlehem, mere miles outside of the town where the Lord was born, in a spot where a conflict of global consequence attains an almost crystalline particularity, lives Daoud Nassar, a Christian whose response to all that has befallen him and his family is, *We refuse to be enemies*. This motto, translated into English, Arabic, Hebrew and German, emblazons large stones at the front gate, welcoming every battle-weary visitor to a sanctuary from the pervasive stink of a conflict that seems all-consuming. The conflict has a readily scripted role for the Nassars to play, but they have declined the part and are writing a different story with their lives.

Western Christian ears do not readily hear an Arabic name and envision a brother in the Lord, but Daoud (the Arabic version of David) is an evangelical Lutheran, and he and his family are active members of Christmas Church in Bethlehem, where Jesus Christ's disciples have lived and prayed in a line unbroken since Pentecost. A gravestone on his farm celebrates his father, Bishara, whose name is Arabic for "the gospel," making Daoud both the biological and spiritual child of the good news. He appears ordinary at first glance—medium in height, close-cropped and gray-streaked black curls, and thick hands and shoulders that contrast with a broad, gentle face. But when he speaks of the land and his stewardship of it, one hears the kingdom of God receiving a living voice.

"We refuse to be victims, because we are not weak," he told our group, while serving us a sun-heated version of traditional Palestinian tea as we gathered in a cave for conversation. "We are in charge."

From a realist's perspective, this statement is patently absurd, coming as it does from a man who has been forced to live underground without running water or electricity and who is surrounded on all sides by would-be enemies. Only two days prior, however, our group had sat together on the Mount of Beatitudes in the north of Galilee and prayerfully read aloud the words Jesus spoke there, recorded in Matthew 5. So our ears were attuned to hear the truth of outlandish claims, declarations that make sense only in the light of a God who took on flesh and demonstrated his power, conquering the world by dying a hideous death on a cross. "Blessed are the poor in spirit . . . the mourners, meek, and merciful . . . those starved and parched for righteousness . . . those with unstained hearts, and those persecuted for the sake of righteousness" (Matthew 5:3-10, paraphrase).

Blessed are these? Nonsense—unless God himself would be crucified. Nonsense—unless God would nail to the cross itself every heavenly and earthly power that causes mourning, unrighteousness, strife. Nonsense—unless God would humiliate sin and death itself with two logs, three nails and his own blood.

Blessed are those who make peace, Jesus said, for they shall be hailed as children of God. At the Tent of Nations farm, this theology takes on flesh. As Daoud is quick to point out, he is fed up with hearing theories about peace and how the Israeli-Palestinian conflict should be resolved. So he has resolved to live out in the present the future resolution and reconciliation that he hopes for. "I believe in small steps," Daoud says. "In this conflict, there is an expectation of how you will react. When you act differently, it confuses people and changes the situation."

This is why, when the soldiers came and knocked down his gate, Daoud met them and asked them what they wanted. They told him they were there to inspect the grounds. "Then," Daoud said, "you are my guests, and you are welcome here. So first we must have tea."

It is almost impossible to overstate the imperative of hospitality in the Semitic cultures of both Israel and Palestine. During our travels in the region, we never stopped without being offered small cups of traditional tea or coffee—sweet, strong and scalding hot—even among the very poor. So Daoud made the soldiers an offer that they quite literally could not refuse. It was the interpersonal version of a computer hack, slicing through the outer conflict that separated them and going straight to a shared cultural source code. The soldiers were confused at first, but found themselves sitting in spite of themselves, and in the act of sipping tea and talking, they were transformed from armed adversaries into guests. Their speech became respectful, as befitting guests, and after finishing the tea, they left without further incident.

Similarly, when the soldiers stopped Daoud's car in the middle of the night and forced him, over his protests, to pull his children from their sleep, he did not return anger for the insult. Instead, he spoke to his children in English, which the soldiers understood as well, saying, "Do not be afraid. These soldiers are people. They are young and frightened like you. They are human beings too. So don't be scared." A change came over the soldiers, and they completed their search quickly. When they finished, the squad commander approached Daoud humbly and spoke to him as a fellow man, rather than a suspected terrorist: "I am sorry that we did that. Please apologize to your children on my behalf."

During our visit to Tent of Nations, one of our group, who pastored one of the most famous churches in the world, gazed over the hilltop through eyes filled with tears. "This is the clearest picture of the kingdom of God," he said, "that I have ever seen." The Tent of Nations has taken its status as a microcosm of the Israeli-Palestinian conflict and, in a bit of theological judo, is living out what it means to choose the way of Jesus Christ over an allegiance to the earthly sides of the battle. They are putting flesh on peace.

Faced with an unrelenting attempt to isolate the farm from the outside world, the Nassars have become pioneers in homesteading and turned their farm into a living laboratory of self-sufficiency. They installed solar panels that soak in the Mediterranean sun and provide twenty-four-hour electricity throughout the property, including electric lights in many of the caves. During the 2009 shelling of Gaza, visible from their land, Daoud and his family channeled their frustration and helplessness into digging another of the now eleven cisterns that collect rainwater and provide a reserve of thousands of liters of water (powered by the solar pump). Four waterless compost toilets stand opposite the pens where egg-bearing chickens and milk-yielding goats cluck and bleat.

And, having been blessed with abundance springing out of seemingly hopeless soil, they are committed to sharing their harvest with Israelis and Palestinians alike. So they run summer camps for youth that bridge religions and nationalities, operate a guest house and job training center for women in the nearby village, and host thousands of visitors annually from around the world.

At the conclusion of our walking tour of the farm, we gathered in the Mountain Chapel—a cave the family discovered in recent years while plowing a field and which visiting groups of volunteers worked to clear and finish. As we entered, the low door compelled our bowing deference to the cross chiseled deep in the massive stone lintel. When our eyes adjusted to the dim light, a circular chapel revealed itself, with chairs and pews ringing a communion table draped in a simple blue cloth, fronted by a wooden pulpit. A stack of Bibles sat ready for takers.

Together we prayed there in thanksgiving for the power of God in that place; for the protection of a humble farm, transformed by grace into a shining city on a hill; and for the courage to trust utterly in God, who in all things works for the good of those who love him—even when no earthly hope offers itself.

O, believer! Do you know that God's power is made perfect in weakness? And do you know that this power did not abandon the world when the last book of the Bible had been written? That it yet rages across our globe, not as a fire or storm or earthquake, but as a still, small voice? That this voice speaks the Word, Jesus Christ? And that the divine Name still brings kings and emperors down from their thrones, knocks warplanes from the air and dismantles tanks, and destroys the division walls—whether built from weak concrete or strong imaginations—that divide us from each other?

BELIEVING IS SEEING

Seeing is believing, we're told, but John 3 reverses the aphorism. Jesus compares the brazen serpent, which heals by being seen, with himself, the Son of Man, who enlivens through belief. There is a connection between seeing and believing—but for John the evangelist, believing is *seeing rightly*.

According to John, humanity has a fundamental perception problem: Jesus "was in the world, and though the world was made through him, the world did not recognize him"—and therefore "did not receive him" (John 1:10-11). In other words, each of us begins in a place of spiritual darkness, with eyes blind from birth, like the man whom Jesus heals in John 9. So, while the brazen serpent was visible on its pole, the Son of Man appears blurry through sin-sick eyes.

But our vision problem is not permanent. Our stumbling progress after God proceeds through a restorative "lifting up" wherein we see better and better, until one day we will finally be given perfect sight. "When Christ appears"—that is, comes again in glory—"we shall be like him, for we shall see him as he is" (1 John 3:2). Importantly, we grow simultaneously in clarity of sight, truth of belief and resemblance to Christ.

"Just as Moses lifted up the snake in the wilderness," Jesus tells Nicodemus, "so the Son of Man must be lifted up, that everyone who believes may have eternal life in him" (John 3:14). By "lifted up," Jesus is clearly speaking about the cross on which he would die. And yet John's Gospel is a subtle text with deep meaning. If we take seriously the connection between *seeing* the serpent and *believing* in the Son of Man, the "lifting up" of Jesus is not only the act of crucifixion but the entirety of his passion, beginning with his interrogation by the Roman governor, Pontius Pilate. For it is Pilate who first holds Jesus up to be viewed by the people, as their ancestors viewed the brazen serpent.

After Pilate has Jesus beaten, his soldiers drape Jesus in a cruel farce of royal garb—a crown of thorns and a borrowed robe of imperial purple—mocking the allegation that he is the Jewish king. Pilate takes Jesus in this sorry state to the gate of his headquarters, that Jesus might be seen by the accusing mob, and makes the declaration similar to what one might expect for the bronze serpent lifted high: "Behold—the man!"

In Pilate, we see a man who often unwittingly declared the truth, in spite of himself, like the sarcastic plaque nailed to the cross, acclaiming Jesus as King of the Jews. This inadvertent service to God's will is consistent with Jesus' observation to Pilate that the Roman governor's authority is an illusion. He unknowingly marches to the purposes of God: "You would have no power over me if it were not given to you from above" (John 19:11).

So it is with Pilate's command for the people to look at Jesus. Behold the man, indeed. As with the brazen serpent lifted high, behold the very image of our sin's consequence: history's only truly innocent man, isolated and alone; slandered and lied about; prosecuted by indifferent powers on trumped-up charges; forsaken by those nearest and dearest, including God himself; betrayed by a friend; bloodied and bruised and swollen from bodily torture; and dressed up in a minstrel-show mockery of greatness, the banal crudeness of which renders it all the more sadistic. This is the Son of Man, the Word of God in flesh and blood, who, like the bronze snake, shows every onlooker the woe we have brought upon our own heads.

Because we are blind to the source of our humanly woe, we do not perceive ourselves in the criminal's dock with Jesus. We do not recognize that he is, in this moment, a mirror perfectly reflecting our true image. So we join with the chief priests and the officials, who declared they would have no king but Caesar, and who shouted, "Crucify! Crucify!"—not knowing that in doing so, we clamor for our own execution. Take this snake away from us.

Those who cry for Jesus' execution imagine that they know how their demand will be met. This man will go to a terrible death on a cross by the road skirting the city, convicted as a rebel, a warning to all who would pick the wrong side in a world squirming under the thumb of imperial power. And that will be the end of that.

But God loves the world by answering our cries according to our need, not our asking. Yes, the Son of Man goes to the very cross that we, not he, deserve. He dies in our place, bearing the wrath of God against our sin. But then this broken and bloodied body, after lying in death for three days, is resurrected into glory. It still bears the marks of torture, so that those who knew Jesus can see the continuity between this life and life eternal, but Jesus is transformed for a kingdom without pain or sorrow.

Those of us on this side of the cross have been given the gift of retrospect. When Pilate introduces Jesus, saying, "Behold the man!" we can recognize two realities: both the fate that we have asked for, which goes to the cross, and the fate that God has opened for all who look on the battered Son of Man and perceive therein the resurrection to eternal life.

Jerusalem has grown since Jesus' day, and the spot outside the city walls where he was crucified is now enveloped by the sprawl of a city at once ancient and modern. If the Tent of Nations represents the distillate of a possible resolution to the current Israeli-Palestinian conflict, twenty-first-century Jerusalem embodies its perpetuation. The city's political fate is the most intractable point in negotiations. As a city sacred to three religions, it is a city of divisions piled on top of divisions. Muslims are not allowed in this area; Jews are not allowed in that one. The oversight of the Church of the Holy Sepulchre, marking the earliest traditional site of Jesus' crucifixion and burial, is divided among six competing Christian traditions, and territorial fistfights and brawls between monks of rival factions are not unheard of.

In other words, Jerusalem is a city of many snakes and many sides, each of which is often far more interested in its own territorial security than in the welfare of the city overall. As our group walked down from the Mount of Ascension, our guide used the city's architecture to illustrate the wounds of more than three thousand years of struggle for the land. We paused to look at the skyline from the spot where Jesus is reputed to have wept over the city. I suspect he would—and does—weep over it today. It is difficult for earthly eyes to look at Jerusalem and see hope for resolution rather than ruin.

Nevertheless, this is the promise of Scripture: at the end, a new Jerusalem will descend to be a center for the people of God. This new city will not emerge from any of our human projects. It is not the culmination of an ideology or program or ideal. It is a pure gift of God, taking what we have broken and bloodied, and transforming it into wholeness, where Christ himself will be our unity. In those days, we will have no trouble seeing, because he himself will be our light.

It is hard to see that Jerusalem over the walls of the city today. It is hard to see the kingdom in the midst of injustice. It is hard to see resurrection in a body of death. Yet this is the only promise worth holding on to. And in certain places, like a farm on a hilltop outside Bethlehem, the kingdom comes close enough that even the most myopic of the faithful can begin to discern its outlines.

- Part two -

A DEEPER CALLING

6

THE PEACEABLE KINGDOM

Moving Toward a Calling

The second half of this book maps out what it means to pursue the kingdom of peace, as described in the vision of the prophet Micah (4:1-5). The shift in focus from a world-saving activism to Micah is basic but fundamental. Instead of a vision of fixing the world we've got, Micah shows us the redeemed kingdom made possible by the cross of Christ, toward which God draws all of history. As Christians, we live in light of this promised new world.

The proposal here is twofold. First, it is that the contours of the coming kingdom call to us from the future, like the memory of a reality that doesn't yet exist. When we respond to this call, the present is shaped as an echo or shadow or trace of what will be. Chapters seven through nine focus on different aspects of this future-oriented memory.

Second, as I explore in chapter ten, Christian activism is most faithful when it is channeled through a sense of calling. I have walked in activist circles long enough to recognize the common sense of anxiety and freneticism that permeates the discipline, as if the fate of the world hangs in the balance of our efforts. In contrast, the

Christian calling is grounded in the peace that comes with accepting our limitations and finitude—an acceptance that allows us to pour ourselves out in divine service.

Both of these ideas are grounded in the conviction that the only solution to the human condition is peace: beginning with God, through Christ, and extending to saturate every aspect of existence.

WELCOMING THE KINGDOM FROM A DISTANCE

I grew up hearing about beating swords into plowshares. This fragment of biblical poetry is a favorite of every peace activist, religious or not, and frequently gets grafted into speeches and articles as a bit of rhetorical flair. The public grounds of the United Nations, a peace-seeking institution, features at least two references to it. One is a large inscription of the passage from the prophet Isaiah. The other is on a dramatic and visibly Soviet statue, donated by the USSR in 1959, under then-premier Khrushchev, who had presided over the Soviet testing of the hydrogen bomb only four years prior. Go figure.

I remember how surprised I was when I first encountered the rich theological context that grounds the passage. The prophets Isaiah and Micah, who prophesied at the same time in Israel's history, record the words as part of a glorious promise of restoration (Isaiah 2:4; Micah 4:3). As the Israelites peered down the dark tunnel of the war that brought the destruction of their nation and exile to Babylon, prophecies of peace and justice to come would have seemed like an impossibly distant light.

The context of the original words reminds us that the promise of peace is rooted in the judgment of the present fall. Micah excoriates the powers in Jerusalem, likening the rulers to cannibals "who eat my people's flesh . . . chop them up like meat for the pan," and paints the false prophets in ways eerily prescient of corrupt televangelists: "They proclaim 'peace' if they have something to eat, but prepare to wage war against anyone who refuses to feed them." Because of these, Micah says, "Zion will be plowed like a field, Jerusalem will become a heap of rubble, the temple hill a mound overgrown with thickets" (3:3, 5, 12 NIV 2011). Given the importance of the temple to Israelite spirituality, these words were tantamount to saying that the politicians and court prophets would be responsible for bringing about the end of the world.

And then, with no warning or transition, Micah delivers one of the Bible's richest pictures of the kingdom of God. We see a densely painted picture of the kingdom—a new order of the world at peace under the reign of Jesus Christ.

> In the last days
> the mountain of the LORD's temple will be established
> as chief among the mountains;
> it will be raised above the hills,
> and peoples will stream to it.
> Many nations will come and say,
> "Come, let us go up to the mountain of the LORD,
> to the house of the God of Jacob.
> He will teach us his ways,
> so that we may walk in his paths."
> The law will go out from Zion,
> the word of the LORD from Jerusalem.
> He will judge between many peoples
> and will settle disputes for strong nations far and wide.
> They will beat their swords into plowshares
> and their spears into pruning hooks.
> Nation will not take up sword against nation,
> nor will they train for war anymore.
> Every man will sit under his own vine
> and under his own fig tree,

and no one will make them afraid,
for the LORD Almighty has spoken.
All the nations may walk in the name of their gods;
we will walk in the name of the LORD
our God for ever and ever. (Micah 4:1-5)

Some might ask what Micah 4 has to say to us today. After all, the prophet's vision remains decidedly future tense: "In the last days," Micah begins, "the mountain of the LORD's temple will be established as chief among the mountains." Is such a vision of peace any more than a glorious promise of those latter days, which we can gaze at for a time before turning back to the tragedies and grim realities of our present condition? What meaning could such a passage have for our war-stricken world?

The example of the Old Testament saints has something to teach us about patiently living in the state of promise. Unlike Abraham, Isaac and Jacob, the people of God today have received the promise of the coming Messiah and have been "marked in him with a seal, the promised Holy Spirit, who is a deposit guaranteeing our inheritance until the redemption of those who are God's possession" (Ephesians 1:13-14). But like them, we also wait, for the second coming of Christ and the consummation of God's kingdom.

So how did they do it? The Old Testament saints were "still living by faith when they died. They did not receive the things promised; they only saw them and welcomed them from a distance, and they admitted that they were aliens and strangers on earth" (Hebrews 11:13). They saw the things promised and "welcomed them from a distance."

To welcome the kingdom from a distance means that it becomes relevant and present to our current situation. Like Abraham, we dwell in the unfulfilled space of God's pledge, "in the promised land like a stranger in a foreign country" (Hebrews 11:9). There is a reason that the book of Acts calls Christians followers of the Way. The life of discipleship is a life of wandering; we live in temporary dwellings in a kingdom that is promised but not yet delivered. A single taut line, stretched between the cross and the coming kingdom, holds up the canvas of our tents.

The vision of Micah 4 will be fulfilled only in the last days, which God alone can bring about. In those days, God's kingdom will be complete because his sovereignty and rule over all things will be made manifest and real, as depicted by the promise that "the mountain of the LORD's temple will be established as chief among the mountains." There will no longer be any denying God as the ruler of the universe. From this recognition of God's rule come all the other attributes of peace outlined in Micah 4. Without the triumph of God, peace on earth is impossible.

Sadly, we don't live in those days. But the lives of Christians in the interim are still a real foretaste of what is to come. This is why Jesus could say that the kingdom had "come near" and "come upon" his followers, while also clearly proclaiming a future consummation of the same. Jesus taught that he himself is the temple of God (John 2:21), and in Christian churches and the lives of Christian believers, "the mountain of the LORD's temple," which is Jesus, is already "established as chief among the mountains." Though our personal exaltation of Jesus Christ, in faith, may be only a shadow of the exaltation to come, our lives should yield the shadows of the fruits of peace that will be fully harvested in the kingdom. This theology does not allow for apathy or indifference to present injustice and lack of peace.

It is important to understand that the continuity between present shadow and future reality is a continuity of *orientation*. As described in Hebrews 12, our situation is like someone who sees a city far off in the distance and starts walking toward it. Our orientation is the city—we take steps toward it, rather than in any of the other directions available to us. It is our goal and our true north, and one day God will bring us to live in the place that we have only seen from far away. We are not pursuing one destination only to discover that God's intention is something else altogether.

However, the fact that we can travel in the right direction does not mean that we can arrive at the city through our own effort. Between the city and us lies the impassable final judgment of God. Unless God brings us there, we will walk toward the city our entire lives without ever arriving. In fact, we will walk toward the city without getting a single step closer to it than when we began. Similarly, the kingdom of God will not be built step by step or brick by brick out of our earthly labors.

When you make a decision to go to a place, you hold your destination in your heart. You incorporate it into your intention. Today, followers of Jesus Christ see Mount Zion in the distance, the mountain of the temple of the Lord, exalted above all other mountains. We have decided to travel in that direction and have become pilgrims on that way.

In the present, therefore, our actions should yield good deeds whose orientation is directed toward God's kingdom. In other words, wherever Jesus Christ is exalted today, the world should start to look a little bit more like Micah 4, revealing an earth fashioned after heaven's pattern.

MAVERICK

I was eight years old when *Top Gun* put my hometown of San Diego on the map. It's not that nobody knew about America's Finest City, as we like to call it; our beaches and what may be the world's most perfect climate had already made San Diego a destination. But with *Top Gun*, the world got a glimpse of a city that lived and breathed the US Navy in the 1980s.

Along with every other kid in San Diego, I loved *Top Gun* instantly. How could I not? Among my small circle of best friends, half of the moms and dads were engaged in the Navy as officers, enlisted sailors or civilian support. My father worked for several decades as a computer programmer for the Navy, first at companies with military contracts and then, at the end of his career, as a civil servant employed directly by the Department of Defense. *Top Gun* was a two-hour celebration of our people, whether they flew F-14s or not.

Yet, despite the near purity of hometown pride and patriotic zeal that *Top Gun* generated in me, I also felt a nagging discomfort at the film's violence, like a barely audible, high-pitched whine or a trace of static. This doubtlessly came from my exposure to my parents' antinuclear activism. In a city that was then profoundly politically conservative, I was self-conscious of my family's "liberal" leanings.

Like any eight-year-old boy, I thrilled at trips with my Cub Scout troop to visit the Navy ships moored in San Diego harbor, where we marveled at gun barrels big enough to stick our heads into, state-of-the-art electronics and the almost unimaginable expanse of an aircraft carrier's deck. But on such trips I also thought about the purpose of those guns, those electronics, that deck, and I wondered without joy what it would be like to be on the receiving end of their fury.

Experiences like this left me with a twinge at *Top Gun*'s scenes of Soviet MiG fighter planes being blown out of the sky. Despite director Tony Scott's clear attempt to dehumanize the dogfight by giving the Soviet pilots opaque, full-face masks, I couldn't help but think about how, hidden in the heart of each exploding plane, some Russian mother's son burned. I knew better than to share such speculations with my fellow Scouts.

The child's tension that I carried must have been nothing next to that of my father. For the duration of his career, he held a Top

Secret security clearance, which means I still don't know how he spent his days; I know only that it involved submarine communications. From nine to five, Monday through Friday, he was actively and intimately involved in the nation's capacity to wage war. In his off hours, he worked to create alternatives to violent conflict. This was hard. In *Top Gun*-era San Diego, a commitment to peace was often disparaged as weak and naïve—and even treasonous. (It's worth noting that the government, which certainly knew of my parents' activism, still always gave my father a security clearance.) Reflecting as an adult, the example of my parents' courage fills me with pride and gratitude.

THE POSSIBILITY OF PEACE

When I became a Christian, I discovered that San Diegans were not alone in their allergy to peace. Many Christians felt it too—or at least the evangelicals I fell in with, and with whom I still make my home.

It was easy to see why theologically and politically conservative Christians found peace suspicious and a little squishy. They knew that an aging ex-hippie sat somewhere in Berkeley, sporting a tie-dye shirt with the words "I'm not as THINK as you STONED I am!" and flashing his fingers in the V-shape of the peace sign. This man represented everything that they believed had gone wrong with America, beginning in the 1960s. During the cultural upheaval of the Vietnam era and its aftermath, traditionalists associated the peace movement with appeasing communism, illegal drug use, loose morals and the decay of traditional society. Peace was found guilty by association and became a concern of "the other side"—the secular humanists, the liberals and so on.

Unfortunately, when Christians disdain peace, it is a clear triumph of cultural religion over biblical fidelity, because peace is at the core of what it means to follow Jesus. Jesus is the "Prince of

Peace" (Isaiah 9:6). The good news that he died for sinners is itself the "gospel of peace" (Ephesians 6:15), because the purpose of the cross was to "[make] peace through his blood" (Colossians 1:20). His peace is to "rule" among us, "since as members of one body you were called to peace" (Colossians 3:15).[1] And, though Paul begins his letters to the churches by pairing "grace and peace," I wonder if most of us hear far more about grace than peace from our churches' pulpits. Despite the clear biblical witness, many Christians resist peace.[*]

Some might reply that I am confusing terms—that the movement to end the war in Vietnam was not the same as the spiritual peace the New Testament describes. Doesn't Jesus say explicitly that he didn't come to bring peace (Matthew 10:34; Luke 12:51) and that he does not give peace as the world gives it (John 14:27)? These statements of Christ do not condemn peace overall, however, but acknowledge that absolute loyalty to the Lord of lords will cause earthly conflict and persecution.

Peace is more than the absence or cessation of war. (The positive vision of peace, painted with a biblical palette, will be the subject of the next three chapters.) But neither does Jesus allow us simply to spiritualize peace. Though the peace of Christ is internal, it does not remain internal. Otherwise, how can we make sense of his exaltation in the Beatitudes of the highly active work of the "peacemaker," which literally combines the Greek words for "peace" and "to make or create" (Matthew 5:9)?

---

[*]Fairness and honesty here demand the acknowledgment of Christians who never gave up on the idea in the first place, such as the traditional "peace churches," like the Anabaptists, along with many mainline Protestant and Roman Catholic churches. One of the less attractive traits of us evangelicals is our "discovery" of trends and ideas that have been around for decades, if not millennia, which we then adopt as if nobody else had ever thought of them before. The current market saturation of "justice" among younger Christians (though welcome) provides a case in point.

Jesus does not bless the peace-feelers or the peace-talkers, but the peace-doers. In both the teachings of Christ and of Scripture, we see that disciples are called to the dynamic work of conflict resolution. In fact, the concrete practices of Christian believers—such as turning the other cheek, foregoing revenge and praying for enemies—actively interrupt the escalating cycle of sin and violence that Scripture so evocatively illustrates in the boast of Cain's descendent, Lamech: "I have killed a man for wounding me, a young man for injuring me. If Cain is avenged seven times, then Lamech seventy-seven times" (Genesis 4:23-24). The peacemaking work of following Christ inhibits this kind of spiraling decay that we see in the generations between Cain and Lamech. We make peace by refusing to give violence its due, and the world is better for it.

Fortunately, the current justice trend in American Christianity bodes well for peace, since the two are theological fraternal twins (see James 3, Psalm 85), and both suffered in conservative circles in the latter twentieth century. The remembrance of justice as a core gospel concept suggests that peace may be due for a similar rehabilitation. For this to happen, however, we need to understand that the Christian problem with peace, when and where it exists, is not simply about a love of war, but also about a love of the wrong kind of war. And the stakes couldn't be higher.

TRUE WAR

Jesus does not call us to run from conflict. In fact, his call is to a combat that makes our earthly battles petty and insignificant by comparison: he calls us to the True War—the war for peace.

The challenge of the True War is that it inverts everything we think we know about struggle. This battle is not won by achieving domination over others, but by loving sacrifice on their behalf. So Paul could tell the Roman church, no strangers to persecution, not to take revenge for wrongs done, because judgment belongs only to God. Instead, he echoes Jesus' replacement of an eye for an eye with love of enemy: "If your enemy is hungry, feed him; if he is thirsty, give him something to drink. . . . Do not be overcome by evil, but overcome evil with good" (Romans 12:20-21).

But the fact that peace and love are our battle flag and bugle does not mean the combat is any less ferocious. Quite the opposite: Jesus advised an unapologetic ruthlessness with our adversary—our own sin. The Sermon on the Mount is no gentle discourse. Certain passages have all the ring of a Marine drill sergeant pacing in front of troops: "If your right eye causes you to sin, gouge it out and throw it away. . . . And if your right hand causes you to sin, cut it off and throw it away. It is better for you to lose one part of your body than for your whole body to go into hell" (Matthew 5:29-30).

Our soft spot for earthly violence can distract us from developing the hard and merciless discipline necessary to wage spiritual combat. Scripture cautions against confusing these categories: "Our struggle is not against flesh and blood, but against . . . the powers of this dark world and against the spiritual forces of evil in the heavenly realms" (Ephesians 6:12).

As pastor and author John Piper says, "There is a mean, violent streak to the true Christian life. Now, let's carefully ask, violence against whom, or what? Not other people. Not other people . . . but on every impulse in our soul to be violent to other people . . . and everything in us that would make peace with sin."[2] Why is it that we can be so amateurish with peace and so professional with our earthly war? What would our faith look like if we approached the business of peace with the life-and-death seriousness and discipline of combat training?

The paradox of the war for peace is that it is not ours to win. Christians often talk about "kingdom building," but no territory we can claim and no edifice we can construct will conquer enduringly for God. The kingdom of God will not be built through incremental human gains, but only by the will of God in finally creating new heavens and a new earth.

So, do our actions in the present matter at all? Yes!—though, again, not in the way we are usually inclined to think.

In the occupied Palestinian territory of Bethlehem, a Christian named Zoughbi al-Zoughbi runs the Palestinian Conflict Resolution center, called Wi'am, which is Arabic for "love." Bethlehem is safe for visitors, but in many ways it is a war zone, bearing all the tactical markers of earthly conflict: barriers and soldiers and brutally efficient weaponry.

In contrast, Wi'am incarnates kingdom battle tactics, waging war for the hearts of citizens who have fallen victim to the traumas and pressures of the ongoing regional tensions. By providing opportunities for women, youth and children, as well as serving as facilitators of a traditional form of Arab mediation, Zoughbi and the Wi'am team temporarily claim both time and space with acts of love. (Their work earned them a prestigious World Vision Peacemaking Award.) Such tactics fly in the face of everything we know about war, which seeks domination. It reflects the theological recognition that God is Lord forever, and we are merely temporary sojourners.

There is no square inch of earth that we may claim permanently for the kingdom of God. Our will may falter. Another may come and use what we have built for sin. The only territory that has been irrevocably determined for the coming kingdom is the body of the Lord Jesus Christ. Faith and prophecy will pass away, Paul writes. But love will not fail. The time and space that we claim today in love will, in fact, persist in the world to come—and it will do so only because the act of love is the act of being formed in the image of the eternal one who loved perfectly and is perfect love, Jesus Christ.

Zoughbi says that love is risk—the dangerous act of caring for another who might hurt us. Few statements better summarize the incarnation, God's taking on flesh for the sake of a world that would nail him to a cross. Because of the risky love of the incarnation, we can love without fear.

A great divide yawns between our fallen present and the kingdom of God. We cannot cross it. But in Jesus Christ, our Lord and savior, teacher and example, we see one who stood in the midst of the fallen orders and was nevertheless perfectly and completely oriented toward the in-breaking kingdom of God. He is the bridge between the two. And he represents the exclusive object of our struggle: to become like him.

Putting the way of Christ and his kingdom into practice requires knowing what that kingdom looks like. The kingdom of God is not simply a blank screen onto which we may project whatever our vision of the good is. Rather, the biblical witness gives a rich testimony to the makeup of the kingdom, allowing us to orient our lives in its direction. What does that look like?

If we read Micah's vision through the lens of the kingdom of peace, three sections emerge. The first is peace with God, which lifts up worship, discipleship and evangelism (Micah 4:1-2). The second is peace among the nations (v. 3), which reveals justice, nonaggression and the industry of human flourishing. The third is peace in community, grounded in dignity, prosperity and security (v. 4). We'll take these topics in turn over the next three chapters.

PEACE WITH GOD

Worship, Discipleship, Evangelism

In the last days

the mountain of the LORD's temple will be established
as chief among the mountains;
it will be raised above the hills,
and peoples will stream to it.

Many nations will come and say,

"Come, let us go up to the mountain of the LORD,
to the house of the God of Jacob.
He will teach us his ways,
so that we may walk in his paths."

The law will go out from Zion,
the word of the LORD from Jerusalem.

MICAH 4:1-2

FATHER FORGIVE

On Christmas Day 1940, Dick Howard stepped in front of a BBC microphone in the midst of his ruined cathedral and surrendered to the peace of God.

The previous month, at nightfall on November 14, Germany had launched Operation Moonlight Sonata, a raid on the city of Coventry, in the United Kingdom's West Midlands.[1] It was something of a miracle that the eleven-hour bombing, which employed both incendiaries and conventional explosives, killed as few as it did: about six hundred confirmed fatalities, with as many as an additional four hundred lost to the flames and many more injured. During the bombing, Howard, who served as the cathedral's provost, or senior clergyman, had joined others in trying to smother incendiary bombs with sand before being driven to find safety.

Coventry, famous for its industry, had been decimated in a single night—including its medieval cathedral, St. Michael's. The German communiqué after the bombing noted that factories "and other targets of military importance" had suffered extensive damage.[2] The bombing gave a name to the new practice of complete aerial destruction of cities: *coventriren,* "to coventrate." Both sides escalated use of city bombing through the war, reaching a climax in the firebombings of Dresden and Tokyo, and finally in the atomic bombs that destroyed Hiroshima and Nagasaki.

A photograph captured King George VI's visit to the cathedral two days after the bombing. He stands with Howard, saying something to him, while a crowd of people in civilian and military dress mills uncertainly around them. Each individual is gazing in a different direction, suggesting the panoramic scope of the devastation, with shattered glass and masonry wherever their eyes might land. Provost Howard stands rigid, his jaw visibly clenched and his eyes fixed on the ground before him as he listens to his king. His hand forms a fist, fingers white-knuckled around his thumb. He looks like a man who feels far from the kingdom of peace.

Howard had a fateful decision to make. The question was not about what action to take: mere hours after the bombing, he had publicly declared that the cathedral would be rebuilt. The question was the spirit in which the rebuilding would occur. It would have been easy for Howard to harden his heart and raise a voice of righteous retribution. He would have made a compelling figure to unify the nation and invoke the wrath of God against the enemy.

But the cathedral community found itself repeatedly called to the foot of the cross. From atop the cathedral's tower, which astonishingly remained standing, the cathedral mason saw two charred timbers lying across each other. He tied them together and erected the cross behind the plain stone table that had been set up where the shattered high altar had stood. A local minister named Arthur Wales found three giant medieval nails, bound them together into another cross and laid it on the new altar. And at some point Howard unclenched his fist, took a piece of chalk and scrawled on the wall behind the altar the words of the crucified Christ: "FATHER FORGIVE."

In Howard's Christmas Day message six weeks later, he incarnated Paul's injunction not to take revenge and showed the listening world, embroiled in war, the peace-bearing fruits of the gospel: "We want to tell the world . . . that with Christ born again in our hearts today, we are trying, hard as it may be, to banish all thoughts of revenge. . . . We are going to try to make a kinder, simpler, a more Christ-Child-like sort of world in the days beyond this strife."[3] The rebuilding of Coventry Cathedral would not be complete until 1962, but Dick Howard lived to see his vision for reconciliation become an integral part of the cathedral's architecture and the congregation's spiritual DNA.

The cathedral stands today as both a building and a community that embody what it means to welcome from a distance Micah's kingdom vision of peace with God. First, it is built around the *worship* of God, who first made peace with us. Second, the cathedral *disciples* believers in God's ways of peace. Third, Coventry is oriented outward in its *evangelism*, spreading God's peace through the gospel of love and grace. And, despite its very specific history, Coventry Cathedral holds universal lessons about finding peace with God.

WORSHIP

Every year over the long Labor Day weekend, I participate in the Council for Christian Approaches to Defense and Disarmament. The meeting rotates annually among the participants' countries, primarily NATO members, and the Sunday is traditionally given over to worship at a local church and a field trip to a site of historical interest—usually a battlefield. In 2011, we met in Birmingham, England, and on Sunday we headed to nearby Coventry to worship in the cathedral.

The cathedral complex offered an initial impression that testifies to resurrection, because the ruined, burned walls of the medieval cathedral still stood, adjacent to the new cathedral. The courtyard between them integrated the two buildings in a powerful visual testimony.

As we approached the building, the massive bronze statue of the Archangel Michael and the devil, mounted over the entry steps of the new cathedral, reinforced this sense of the triumph of good over evil. Nearly twenty feet high, Michael appears to hover over the figure of Satan, who lies with feet chained and arms bound. The archangel's outstretched fists and flaring wings extend over the heads of visitors. In one hand, he holds an immense spear.

I watched groups of visitors arrive and saw as their eyes were drawn up to the angel's impassive, slightly sorrowful face. The message was clear and unsettling for the unrepentant sinner in each of us: spiritual war is real, and the judgment of God triumphs.

The statue was just a foretaste, though. At the top of the stairs, we entered the cathedral through doors in an etched glass wall seventy feet high and forty-five feet wide. Alternating rows of saints and flying, trumpeting angels, etched freehand by a single artist, cover the window and appear to be moving as the light hits the panes. As we stared up at triumphant angels, saints and martyrs, we could see the reflection of the old cathedral's ruined walls behind us and the interior of the new cathedral before us.

This translucent storm of angels and saints brought to mind the invitation of Hebrews 12:1-2: "Since we are surrounded by such a great cloud of witnesses, let us throw off everything that hinders and the sin that so easily entangles, and let us run with perseverance the race marked out for us. Let us fix our eyes on Jesus, the author and perfecter of our faith, who for the joy set before him endured the cross, scorning its shame, and sat down at the right hand of the throne of God." So we found ourselves placed bodily in visceral reminders of the fall, the saints and the kingdom to come—and we hadn't even set foot in the building yet!

The most important lesson was yet to come. We'd arrived about a half hour prior to the start of the services, so we had a chance to walk around and see the cathedral's marvelous architecture and artwork. One of the best features was the series of stained-glass windows along the walls, which shone with color and depicted the Christian journey from creation to the fall—faithfulness, suffering, death and resurrection into eternal life. The layout of the windows puzzled me, though: the cathedral walls were not straight, but instead had a curious saw-tooth shape, angling in and out, and the windows were on the angle facing toward the altar, away from the entryway. This meant that they were invisible to anyone in the pews; you would have to turn around in your seat to see them, which seemed a shame to me.

As a Baptist, it didn't occur to me that the cathedral was built around the movement of Anglican worship. In the Anglican service, the minister often walks the Gospel book into the center of the congregation and proclaims the Scripture there. As the Word of God moves through the congregation, worshipers turn to face it.

I didn't know that the liturgy was the building's secret. While the Coventry worship service went on, I forgot about the stained glass—until the Gospel reading. As the congregation turned, however, we could see the brilliant morning sun kaleidoscoping through the stained-glass windows along the walls, lighting the etched angels and saints in the rear wall as if they were bodies of fire. The riot of color and white light blinded my eyes, which had adjusted to the cathedral's interior, while the words of Scripture filled my ears. As I would see later, the fullest picture of all was saved for after communion—for only after walking forward to take the bread and the cup is the worshiper able to see all the stained glass, the complete journey of amazing grace to the kingdom's end.

The point of all this is not that a visitor to Coventry Cathedral will likely have a unique and exceptional worship experience. The point is not the experience at all. Worship is not a means to some other goal, like evangelism—that is, we don't put on a great show on Sunday as a way of drawing people in. Rather, worship is the primary end of Christianity itself, in our adoration and praise of the God who reveals himself to us in the gospel of Jesus Christ. Coventry Cathedral incarnates the worship we see in Micah—"the mountain of the LORD's temple will be established as chief among the mountains"—by proclaiming the incomparable Christ and his gospel to all who worship there.

The person of Christ saturates every inch of the sanctuary—perhaps most dramatically in the tapestry, *Christ in Glory*, that covers the wall behind the altar. It was the largest tapestry in the world when it was hung, but even more remarkable than its size is its subject. Christ seated in heaven, surrounded by the beasts of Revelation that symbolize the four Gospels, is not the sort of polite Jesus, meek and mild, that you find in many churches. This cosmic Christ rules Coventry Cathedral, peerless and overwhelming, bursting with the promise of judgment to come.

Yet the image also draws an explicit connection between crucifixion and glorification. The base of the tapestry depicts a crucified Jesus who, though still larger than life, is dwarfed by the glorified Christ above. But this does not diminish the cross, because the woven crucifixion hangs level with the altar. The worshiper going forward to receive Communion looks over the altar to see the sacrifice that the table symbolizes—ensuring that no one will "eat and drink without discerning the body of Christ" (1 Corinthians 11:29 NRSV). In this sense, the tapestry mirrors the incarnation: the Son of God who took on flesh for our sake is at our level, while the towering Christ in glory overhead reminds the worshiper that the crucified Jesus is the "power of God and the wisdom of God" (1 Corinthians 1:24) and that, as we "share in his sufferings" through communion, we "also share in his glory" (Romans 8:17).

The tapestry also resolves the tension caused at the cathedral's entry. The old cathedral's ruined walls and the statue of the Archangel Michael and the devil are a visible reminder that evil is a present reality. These do not leave in question which side wins: the new cathedral looms over the old and a fierce Michael dominates the bound devil. The sides seem close enough, though, that you know it's been a fight.

But the enthroned Christ on the tapestry puts everything in perspective. On his left side, at about knee level, two tiny figures grapple—the only asymmetric element in the tapestry—showing Michael casting Satan out of heaven (Revelation 12:7-9). In the external statue, both Michael and the devil dwarf the human form, and you feel lucky that Michael has the edge. On the tapestry, however, both are insignificant compared to the enthroned Christ—they aren't even as big as any one of the Gospels symbolized. The message is clear: though in our day evil abounds and often seems on the verge of winning, in the scale of the kingdom, it's barely an afterthought, let alone a competitor.

How liberating it was for an activist-minded Christian like me to see and remember that we do not fight our battles on a level field. Our perception of good and evil as evenly matched adversaries is based on the skewed perception of our fallen vision. But we have distorted optics, like a carnival mirror, that magnify evil and diminish Christ. From a kingdom perspective, evil dwindles to its true insignificance and Christ erupts in his unfathomable splendor. This means that our battle is not nearly so much against the adversary. It is rather with whatever prevents us from seeing Jesus Christ in his complete glory—as we do when we worship in truth.

DISCIPLESHIP

Micah's vision is particularly enthusiastic about learning: different peoples will come together and say, Let's go to the temple of the God of Jacob! For "he will teach us his ways, so that we may walk in his paths" (Micah 4:2). The apostolic term for this practice of instruction is *catechesis*, which appears in the New Testament as "instruction"—such as the description of the famous preacher Apollos as one who "taught about Jesus accurately" (Acts 18:25). A broader contemporary term might be *discipleship*, referring to education (learning the ways of God) that translates into action (that we may walk in his paths).

Throughout church history, most Christians could not read—and wouldn't have had a Bible in their language even if they had been literate—so their exposure to the gospel of Christ was primarily aural. But church buildings and cathedrals came to play an equally important educational role through their visual depiction of biblical stories. The importance of such "gospel architecture" can be hard to comprehend in a contemporary North American church context, where function often trumps form—if the latter gets any attention at all. But for the majority of Christian history, art has been critical to the discipleship of simple and devout believers.

The new Coventry Cathedral stands solidly in the lines of its medieval forebears, with the building itself teaching and proclaiming the gospel. In addition to the core instruction of worship, the cathedral disciples in several other ways, most notably in three smaller spaces that stick out from the core, like spokes on a wheel: the Altar of Reconciliation, the Unity Chapel and the Chapel of Christ the Servant. Together, these three features communicate core Christian practices—the ways in which we walk in response to the gospel of peace—of *reconciliation, unity* in Christ, and life as *vocation*. I'll take each in turn below.

DISCIPLESHIP: *Reconciliation*

The work of reconciliation begins by looking into the face of the damage done. As noted above, the new cathedral was built with its front entry opening onto the ruins of the medieval building. The spiritual significance of maintaining the old walls as a sort of antechamber to the new cathedral was immediately apparent to Basil Spence, the architect who won the rebuilding design competition: "I saw the old cathedral as standing clearly for the Sacrifice, one side of the Christian Faith, and I knew my task was to design a new one which would stand for the Triumph of the Resurrection. . . . In these few moments the idea of the design was planted."[4]

The old ruins, open to the sky, have been cleared of debris and now regularly house worship. The centerpiece is the Reconciliation Altar, which Dick Howard and others built in the immediate aftermath of the bombing. Jock Forbes's charred cross stands behind it, fronting blown-out windows, and Howard's chalked words, "FATHER FORGIVE," have been etched in gold into the wall.

Many observers note the fragmentary quality of the quote, since Howard left off the end of Jesus' words: "them, for they do not know what they do" (Luke 23:34). So the effect is not that only the German bombers who caused the devastation need forgiveness, but all humanity. A large statue of Christ before Pilate, *Ecce Homo*, looks over the altar space, reminding worshipers of our universal guilt in crucifying God. Unlike Jesus, none of us is an innocent victim.

Each Friday, the altar is the site of the Coventry Litany of Reconciliation, a prayer based on the seven deadly sins, which teaches worshipers the connection between sin, forgiveness and peacemaking. It begins by declaring, "All have sinned and fallen short of the glory of God," and prays, "Father, forgive" in response to each confession. In closing, the litany commands worshipers to extend the grace of the gospel to others: "Be kind to one another, tenderhearted, forgiving one another, as God in Christ forgave you."

The participating congregation is thus prepared to walk in the Christian way of God-centered forgiveness not only when it is easy, but—as the ruined surroundings remind us—even in the midst of devastation. This is the foundation of the Christian life itself: as we plead in the Lord's Prayer, God forgives us our trespasses just as "we forgive those who trespass against us."

DISCIPLESHIP: *Unity*

The way of forgiveness opens up into new community, and the path away from Coventry's outer ruins reflects this discipleship. As you move into the cathedral, the Chapel of Unity opens to the left. This circular space, modeled after the crusaders' ten-sided tent, juts out from the cathedral proper. Given how Coventry Christians crossed denominational lines to work and pray together, the cathedral rebuilders wanted to offer a place within the grounds that could facilitate further expressions of Christian unity.

In that spirit, the chapel door opens onto the spectacular baptistry on the opposite cathedral wall—a floor-to-ceiling wall of rainbow-colored stained glass, with a gold-white sunburst at the center illuminating the baptismal font on the ground in front of it, a hollowed-out boulder from Bethlehem. The Unity Chapel's orientation to the baptistery evokes Ephesians 4:4-6, which reminds Christians that our unity is received from God, not created by our efforts: "There is one body and one Spirit—just as you were called to one hope when you were called—one Lord, one faith, one baptism; one God and Father of all, who is over all and through all and in all."

The chapel's symbolism further reinforces the centrality of Jesus Christ for Christian unity. The mosaic floor depicts symbols of Christ's supremacy: an alpha and omega mark his complete embrace of time; loaves and fishes display his sufficiency for our needs; the world's continents display his global sovereignty. The subtly concave floor tilts every point in the room toward the center, where the image of a dove invokes both Spirit and peace, and recalls the biblical teachings that "as members of one body you were called to peace" (Colossians 3:15) and that we should "make every effort to keep the unity of the Spirit through the bond of peace" (Ephesians 4:3).

The Unity Chapel's consistent allusion to Ephesians 4 brings to mind the scriptural instruction that from Christ "the whole body, joined and held together by every supporting ligament, grows and builds itself up in love, as each part does its work" (Ephesians 4:16). This is a powerful word for a younger generation of activist-minded

Western Christians, who must remember diversity within unity. When we try to do everything ourselves, we risk disrespecting the diversity of gifts that Christ has given to his body.

I remember facilitating a discussion on faith and activism at a conference for university chaplains and ministers. One young woman confessed that she was the consummate "joiner." Give her a Christian cause and something to do, and she was on board. She'd like it on Facebook, follow on Twitter, buy the product, go to the conference, do the small group study. You name it; she'd do it. She was also exhausted, on the verge of burnout. As she spoke, sympathetic heads nodded around the table, including my own.

It struck me that those of us who shared such well-intentioned impulses were actually modeling ourselves after the wrong Christ. Our problem wasn't a lack of concern for Jesus; his heart and compassion drove our response to a fallen world. But in taking the world's burdens onto our backs, we were trying to grow in the image of Christ that we see in Colossians: the cosmic Jesus in whom "all things hold together" and through whose blood God chose to "reconcile to himself all things" (1:17, 19). Horrified by the sin and pain that a firebombed cathedral symbolizes, we try to stretch wide enough and sacrifice hard enough to fix it. Does this sound like the faith of anyone you know?

Our shoulders aren't big enough for that task. The miracle of the incarnation means that Jesus the man is also the Son of God, and so his sacrifice is sufficient for all of us. As disciples, we are called to conformity with his image, but not to his divinity (see Romans 8:29; Luke 6:40). In the student ministers' discussion, Greg Carmer, the Dean of Chapel at Gordon College, put it well: a mature understanding of the unity of the body of Christ allows us to *care* about everything Christ cares about, but to *carry* only what he has given us to bear.

God has predestined us to become "little Christs" as we grow in maturity. Our resemblance to Jesus is like spiritual DNA, wherein all the parts of the body, though different in appearance and function, carry the same essential coding. This doesn't mean that we put our feet up and relax—but how liberating it is to remember that Jesus does not need any help being the head or the whole of the body, and that "each part" can simply focus on doing its own work!

DISCIPLESHIP: *Vocation*

How, then, do we carry what God has called us to? If you leave the Unity Chapel and walk to the far end of the cathedral, the Chapel of Christ the Servant opens to your right. Here the cathedral disciples us into the value of vocation. The chapel is also called the Chapel of Industry as an homage to Coventry's historic status as a center of English commerce and manufacturing. In the Middle Ages, the labor of Coventry's many craftspeople made it England's "fourth city," after London, Bristol and York. The power of medieval industry is still visible in the shape of the ruined cathedral walls, which contained chapels dedicated for the use of particular trade guilds.

Coventry Cathedral has never been one of those churches where the outside world is forgotten, with sharp lines drawn between Sunday morning and the rest of the week. In keeping with the cathedral's Benedictine monastic heritage, the Chapel of Christ the Servant teaches the rhythm of Christian life—*ora et labora*, work and pray— by opening through clear glass windows onto the space of the downtown street outside. The communion vessels, made by local craftspeople, are visible from the street, reminding those on both sides of the windows of the porous border between church and city.

Though vocation is historically associated with calls to church-related or religious ministry, Christians today recognize the value of discerning vocation in all walks of life. The concept of vocation, or calling, is enjoying something of a renaissance in Christian circles. This desire to find the sacred in traditionally secular locations and occupations fits well with the Coventry Cathedral ethos of "the offering of all of human life to God," as former vice-provost Michael Sadgrove writes in a cathedral guidebook.

The Chapel of Christ the Servant identifies the common denominator of every Christian calling: self-sacrificial service. As you cross the chapel's threshold, you walk across Jesus' commandment from the Last Supper—"Now that I, your Lord and Teacher, have washed your feet, you also should wash one another's feet" (John 13:14)—and then you see a circular altar ringed with Jesus' declaration "I am among you as one who serves" (Luke 22:27). Regardless of the work done, what makes a calling a calling is that it is an individual's defining service to God and neighbor.

Paul addresses the roles of husbands and wives, parents and children, and masters and slaves—each a pairing of a person with absolute social power over a person without any power in the ancient Roman context—and then tells them, "Whatever you do, work at it with all your heart, as working for the Lord. . . . It is the Lord Christ you are serving" (Colossians 3:23-24). For Christians, there is no socioeconomic status or occupation that is too great or too menial to be offered as service: the calling of the Lord Jesus himself.

In earlier centuries, particular callings were often exalted as "more spiritual" than others—so a foreign missionary was the greatest, followed by a pastor, followed by a college minister and so on. In some circles today, zeal for foreign missions has ebbed, but if the keynote speaking roles at major Christian conferences are any indicator, we may have simply adopted a new hierarchy that fits an activist faith: NGO or nonprofit leader, church planter, social entrepreneur, micro-financier and so on. But heaven does not smile with particular favor on any of these. The most mundane work, if offered as genuine service to God, is greater by far than a labor that seems outwardly kingdom oriented but is self-glorifying.

EVANGELISM

When time was ripped open and Micah saw the coming kingdom, he saw a day when Jerusalem would be restored to glory and the rule of God would emanate from the holy city. In that kingdom, evangelism will no longer be necessary, of course. Evangelism is a "meanwhile" activity by definition: the proclamation of the gospel that Jesus Christ died for sinners, was raised and will come again to consummate his kingdom. I wonder if career evangelists will take a few minutes to adjust to the kingdom when it comes; they won't have anything to do except point at everything their eyes fall on and holler, "See!" That's how complete God's rule will be. But in these latter days, evangelism is the way we anticipate, or welcome from a distance, the promise of God's universal law in the kingdom.

While I was working out the ideas for this book, I had breakfast with my friend Mark, who works at a Christian magazine. I explained that I wanted to help Christians remember the gospel centrality of peace. "The problem," Mark said, "is that I can't think of a single peace movement that maintains any emphasis on evangelism." His comment stuck with me, and I couldn't think of a counterexample. Unfortunately, the reverse also appears to be true (with apologies to the Mennonites): few evangelistic movements maintain a rigorous emphasis on peacemaking.

So, what gives? Do we want to choose between the gospel of salvation and its effect? But it is a false choice to force a decision between the seed of a tree and its fruit or the mountain spring and the rushing river it feeds. Christ leads to his kingdom. You can't have one without the other. Of course, conversion precedes its effects. But those who think this means that "winning souls" is the only thing that matters are trying to call it quits before their Lord does.

Evangelism is the proclamation of the "gospel of peace"—God reconciling himself to us through the cross. As we saw in the last chapter, Scripture is clear that this peacemaking cannot be spiritualized, but should yield concrete outcomes. Though Jesus will cause conflict, the ultimate effect of the gospel is to make real life more peaceful, in no small part because Christ's followers should prefer to endure suffering rather than to inflict it.

My breakfast with Mark happened before my visit to Coventry, or I would have had a snappy retort. At the close of the Coventry communion service, they blessed a cross of nails that they subsequently sent to Christ Church Cathedral in Hartford, Connecticut—the newest addition to the Community of the Cross of Nails (CCN). The giant medieval nails that Rev. Wales pulled from the rubble and forged into the cross have become an internationally recognized symbol for Christ-centered reconciliation. After World War II ended, the cathedral sent replicas of the nail cross to three German cities that the Allies had heavily bombed during hostilities. The Berlin cross proved especially significant for its ultimate placement in the Kaiser Wilhelm Memorial Church, which, like Coventry Cathedral, was rebuilt next to the bombed-out ruin of its precursor.

Thus began the CCN, a reconciliation ministry that today includes more than 150 partner churches, organizations and institutions in sixty countries, as well as a school-specific initiative called ICONS. Community of the Cross of Nails members, who proclaim their membership by displaying a cross of nails, share in the practice of regularly praying the God-focused, sin-acknowledging, gospel-proclaiming Coventry Litany of Reconciliation and in a passionate commitment to seeing the concrete effects of God's reconciling work, whatever that means in their particular contexts.

The cathedral explains their work in light of 2 Corinthians 5:18-20, which declares that God has "reconciled us to himself through Christ" and has given us "the ministry of reconciliation. . . . We are therefore Christ's ambassadors, as though God were making his appeal through us." At the cathedral, this reconciliation with God comes through a commitment to gospel preaching and worship, along with a variety of evangelistic discipleship programs like Alpha and Christianity Explored. And from Coventry, where Christ is so unapologetically exalted, God's law of peace has spread around the world. Given the history of the bombing and rebuilding, the community views this as their distinct "heartbeat" or "God's thumbprint" on them.

The stated centrality of Christ to the work of reconciliation does not mean that the answer to complex conflict situations is simply to go in and proclaim the lordship of Christ, which makes for neither good peacemaking nor good evangelism. It does mean, however, that external peacemaking is never divorced from the spiritual reconciliation worked in Jesus Christ and that by remembering the gospel of the cross in the midst of peacemaking, the work's ultimate glory is given to God.

COMING DOWN FROM THE MOUNTAIN

My wife and I had moved to Toronto shortly before I made my trip to Coventry, and we hadn't yet found a church home. When I arrived back on my side of the Atlantic, I told her, "I've found a church for us—but it's a killer commute." At Coventry Cathedral, I found a place, history and community living in kingdom anticipation, illustrating Micah's vision of peace with the God who has made peace with us. But it is obviously a very specific example with an exceptional history and calling. What does this example offer to those whose own circumstances bear little to no resemblance to the worship, discipleship and evangelistic witness of this Anglican cathedral in the middle of England?

The good and bad news is that you are the only person who can answer that question. There is a connection to be made, but it takes work and theological imagination. One of the glories of the kingdom of heaven and of the body of Christ that anticipates it is that we'll do things differently depending on where we are: from the artsy quarter of East Nashville to the gentrifying West End of Toronto; from the Atlanta suburbs to the college town of Berkeley; from midtown Manhattan to Brooklyn, a few miles and a world apart. Context matters. Moreover, the point here is not Coventry Cathedral itself, but the way in which it anticipates the kingdom within its own history and setting. How will you do the same in yours?

One way forward is to consider the questions that Coventry raises about the three aspects we've seen in Micah: worship, discipleship and evangelism (such questions apply especially to church leaders, but not exclusively so).

The worship takeaway of Coventry is that kingdom-focused worship isn't about how it makes us feel, and we do ourselves no favors when we talk about it that way: "how was your worship experience?" Worship does not begin with our subjective experience of it but with the God it praises. As the author of Hebrews tells us, we have already arrived: "You *have come* to Mount Zion, to the city of the living God, the heavenly Jerusalem." From this vantage point, "we are receiving"— note it is neither "will receive" nor "have received"—"a kingdom that cannot be shaken." Therefore, says the author, "let us be thankful, and so worship God with reverence and awe" (Hebrews 12:22-29).

So, does every facet of our worship proclaim the God of the gospel, wherever we are? Are there ways in which we could more greatly glorify him? Does our worship fall squarely between confidence in the cross and expectation of the kingdom? Does it allow us room to be transformed by the Spirit, who is bringing the kingdom about? And does our proclamation pass the test of offering our "reverence and awe"?

Regarding discipleship, not every church will feature three separate chapels for instruction in reconciliation, unity and vocation.

But any community wishing to learn God's law of peace and to walk in his ways can evaluate its own practices of discipleship against related criteria. How much of a priority is Christian formation in our contexts? Does the congregation understand formation in Christ's image as one of its primary purposes and does it dedicate its time and resources accordingly—with special attention to the three ways that Coventry highlights?

First, are our churches forgiving? Not a polite, we'll-get-past-it people, but a body genuinely committed to extending the gospel grace that it has received?

Second, concerning unity, do our church members understand that the Christian life is a call to recognize, rather than to create, the unity that Christ bestows? Are we growing in our understanding of ourselves as an integral part of a body, allowing us to exercise our particular gifts freely, trusting and celebrating that others will do the same differently?

And third, do those who are not called to a religious vocation— the vast majority of Christians—understand their weekday lives to be an equal calling of God? Do our churches celebrate the work that their members do in the world as they equip them for "works of service"? Are we able to give a testimony of how we approach our daily lives as a work of service, as if offered to God?

Finally, the question of evangelism may be where Coventry has the most radical input to offer. In practice, churches often seem to make evangelism their sole concern or ignore it altogether. Many Christians find the entire concept profoundly uncomfortable, because evangelism can seem arrogant and presumptuous, not to mention judgmental. I wonder if Coventry might reveal peace as the secret ingredient in reconsidering evangelism.

Frequently, both our attitudes and approaches toward evangelism demonstrate a profound anxiety and freneticism. In the unifying factor of peace, however, we find an alternative approach to the simple "you're going to hell" threat. It requires that we first fully embrace the peace with God that Christ has worked on our behalf. This is still salvation to those who are perishing, but the effect is to focus on the promise of reconciliation with God rather than on the punishment to be avoided. By understanding our salvation in this light, evangelism becomes a welcome invitation into a life of spiritual peace for modern people who live in highly fractured, anxious contexts. It is the same promise that incarnation held for those two thousand years ago: "Glory to God in the highest, and on earth peace, goodwill toward all!" (Luke 2:14).

8

PEACE AMONG THE NATIONS

Justice, Industry, Nonaggression

He will judge between many peoples
and will settle disputes for strong nations far and wide.

They will beat their swords into plowshares
and their spears into pruning hooks.

Nation will not take up sword against nation,
nor will they train for war anymore.

MICAH 4:3

A U-HAUL AT PENNSYLVANIA AND THIRD

Our plane came to a halt on the tarmac, and everybody groaned. The flight had already been delayed several times at the gate and the jetway, and despite the pilot's pledge of imminent takeoff, the promise of a quick wheels-up was rapidly receding. This was not good news to the three-dozen weary souls packed into the snug confines of the Embraer RJ140, the regional jet that American Airlines uses to run short-hop routes like that between Nashville and Washington, DC's Reagan National Airport. We all wanted to make it home to Nashville in time for dinner, but that possibility seemed increasingly unlikely. I leaned back in my seat and gazed out the window.

The view should have been enough to cheer the soul of even the most cynical traveler. Despite having flown in and out of Reagan Airport more times than I can count, the experience never gets old. I always try to get a left-side window seat on inbound flights, with the hopes that the day will be clear and I can enjoy the approach over the Potomac, with Washington's unmistakable monuments coming into view and shining like beacons. Though the takeoff lacks the spectacular gems of the landing, it still has its delights, like the sight then visible from our stationary plane. The Washington Monument rose at the left edge of my view, matched on the right by the towering Capitol dome. The fading sunlight cast both in a gold and pink glow.

As I looked at the glorious evening skyline, I thought, The fireball from a nuclear terrorist bomb would just about fill the sky between them.

If it happens, it goes down something like this: Let's say it is 9:19 p.m. on Tuesday, January 24, 2017, the night of the new president's State of the Union Address. The stolen U-Haul truck exits the Beltway at I-66, crosses the Teddy Roosevelt Bridge and makes a quick jog on E Street to Nineteenth to Constitution Avenue, which dumps out onto Pennsylvania Avenue. It then drives two blocks to the road closure at Third Street, where it turns right and is immediately flagged down by a diligent officer in the Capitol Police, who is suspicious of a cargo van driving around at night. The truck pulls over on Third, next to the National Gallery of Art, and as the officer approaches the driver's side window, the world's first nuclear suicide bomber detonates the small bomb in the cargo hold, less than 1,500 feet from the US Capitol building.

The weapon is the same gun-type design that the United States used on Hiroshima—crude and weak, and inefficient by modern standards. It is also so simple that it did not need to be tested, using conventional explosives to slam one piece of uranium into another, causing a chain reaction that releases energy equivalent to thirty million pounds of TNT.

One millionth of a second after the bomb explodes, the president of the United States is well into his speech. Also in the chamber are the vice president and the Speaker of the House, the Supreme Court, the president's cabinet, the Joint Chiefs of Staff, virtually every congressperson, the president's family and several eminent US business and civic leaders, whom the president plans to recognize in his address. He has just delivered an early applause line, so the members of his party are all standing and clapping. Then everybody in the room is killed.

The US Capitol is basically a big block of stone, but it is enveloped by a fireball about as hot as the sun and struck by a blast wave that delivers approximately 15 psi (pounds per square inch) of force to the building. This sort of pressure can destroy fortifications, never mind quake-resistant buildings.

The fireball and blast spread in every direction from the hypocenter. They encompass and destroy most congressional and senate offices; the Supreme Court and Library of Congress; the headquarters for the Internal Revenue Service and the Federal Bureau of Investigation; the Departments of Energy, Commerce and Transportation; and several Smithsonian museums. Beyond the immediate blast, unreinforced buildings collapse from Fourteenth Street Northwest to Fifth Street Southeast, with shattered windows and debris turning a two-mile radius into a giant shrapnel field. Viewed from above, it looks like Satan has ground out his cigar on the face of the earth.

A cloud of irradiated ash, dust and debris rises from the Capitol and blows southwest toward the Virginia suburbs. Those who take shelter in a basement or interior room of a reinforced building radically increase their odds of survival.* Most people don't. They panic, flee, receive a critical level of radiation exposure, get violently ill and die.

Beyond the immediate crisis itself and the scores of thousands of lives lost, the extended consequences of the attack unravel life and the world as we know it. The economic effects are the most far ranging: border shutdowns destroy global shipping, with the financial markets following after, and economies collapse under the weight of skyrocketing prices and resource scarcity, especially energy.

The incineration of the National Archives' Charters of Freedom—the original copies of the Declaration of Independence, the Constitution and the Bill of Rights—are more than symbolic; this is the equivalent of a national near-death experience, and people demand tyranny for the safety it promises. The bombers have chosen governmental decapitation over sheer casualties; the same bomb in Times Square or in DC during business hours could have killed hundreds of thousands more. But in one stroke the national governing apparatus of the United States has been decimated.

The secretary of transportation, an unelected former industry executive who was at a secure location during the speech in case of precisely such an event, becomes president of a nation on the verge of global nuclear war. He assumes an executive office suddenly vested with extraordinary powers by the popular mandate for limitless vengeance. There is no telling what our nation, exploding in rage and pain, will do in response to such an attack.

The temptation is to find some guilty party to punish in like manner, even if that means destroying the innocent inhabitants of whatever countries can be determined to have offered the bombers material support. Those who speak out against the slaughter of in-

---

*For information about nuclear preparedness, visit knowshelter.com.

nocents are shouted down as traitorous, if not officially silenced. God help our church in that day, because Christians, spiritually unprepared for this level of suffering, join the chorus for vengeance. When terrible vengeance is finally ours, whatever is left of the world will have no interest in hearing the gospel from the lips of a people who could sanction the things we do.

I think about this future every day, not just when I am looking out my window from the tarmac at Reagan National. More often than not, I am convinced that it or another like it—or worse (the consequences of a small nuclear war between India and Pakistan are beyond description)—will happen, mainly because we know the actions we need to take to prevent it but cannot seem to muster the collective willpower to do them, and so we drift along a river of sloth and pride toward catastrophe.

I hate this future with every cell in me. There is nothing that would so comprehensively destroy aspirations toward justice, industry and nonaggression in our day. Faced with such possibilities, the promise of Micah 4 will break your heart, if you'll let it. It tells of an era when the *justice* of God will adjudicate between strong nations and many peoples. It pledges that we will someday devote our *industry* toward instruments of human flourishing rather than destruction. It foresees a time utterly *lacking in aggression* between one people and another. Looking through this biblical lens, we can see what it means to anticipate these facets of the kingdom in our own day.

JUSTICE

Micah tells of a day when God "will judge between many peoples and will settle disputes for strong nations far and wide," and the kingdom trait of *justice* stands as the preeminent requirement for peace among the peoples. In American Christian circles, a renewed commitment to the gospel centrality of justice has gone mainstream in recent years. (We should note that many churches and parachurch organizations never forgot about justice in the first place.) This revival is due in no small part to the efforts of one former Justice Department lawyer, Gary Haugen, who founded the International Justice Mission (IJM) in 1997 and wrote *Good News About Injustice* (that is, "God is against it") to help a largely indifferent evangelical audience rehabilitate the faith's historic commitment to justice in an individualistic church culture.

Today, IJM fields lawyers all over the world who are doing the focused work of seeking justice for victims of slavery, trafficking and other violent oppression, as well as accountability for perpetrators. A recent recipient of a record-setting corporate anti-slavery grant from Google, IJM has set the gold standard for a Christian organization working impeccably outside the boundaries of faith-based circles.

For the past decade, the justice revival in American churches has primarily focused on direct injustices against human persons, like slavery and trafficking. As the commitment to justice grows to mainstream maturity, it is already showing signs of recognizing the holistic import of justice, not simply in those areas where it is radically absent, but as a constructive virtue affecting all aspects of life.

This is the sort of broader justice that we see on display in Micah, in which the Lord God adjudicates between peoples and nations. In Micah's vision of peace among peoples, justice is not solely a matter of interpersonal resolution between oppressor and victim. Rather, in addition to being an intrinsic good, justice also serves to prevent war.

Scriptures like Judges 11 help illuminate this meaning. Here, the Israelites have been living in the Promised Land for several hundred years, but are threatened by the king of the Ammonites, who claims that the Israelites took his land when they came up out of Egypt. Jephthah, the Israelite judge and military leader, sees this claim for what it is—an excuse for territorial expansion. "For three hundred years Israel occupied" the land, Jephthah replies, so "why didn't you retake them during that time?" Possession of the land, he argues, is a question of divine might—the God of Israel gave the Israelites the land, and Chemosh, the Ammonite god, has not taken it back. Therefore, Jephthah says, "I have not wronged you, but you are doing me wrong by waging war against me. Let the LORD, the Judge, decide the dispute this day" (Judges 11:23-27). In essence, Jephthah is saying God will vindicate the right side by giving them military victory, and the story ends with the Israelites' triumph.

The battle did not have to take place at all. The king of Ammon knew he was in the wrong—using an ancient grudge as a pretext for a land grab—but he ignored Jephthah's message, presumably because he did not trust in the sovereignty of a foreign God's judgment.

Contemporary readers should be extremely careful how we interpret this story. The moral is not that God has approved of every victor of armed combat. Elsewhere in Scripture, we see military triumph as a precursor to downfall, as with the Babylonians. God's providence is inscrutable, and we see many biblical stories of the wicked and strong oppressing the weak and righteous through force of arms.

The moral of the story is that *all war begins with injustice*—whether real, imagined or claimed. Violence between peoples is not due to some intrinsic, bestial hostility; consider that Cain, the world's first murderer, killed his brother over the perceived injustice of God's preferring Abel's sacrifice over Cain's. So we cannot simply accept war as the unavoidable human condition, though its cause is intimately related to the human condition of sin, from which injustice comes. Nations and peoples war with each other because justice does not reign between them, and they cannot resolve their disputes. They will therefore continue to war until the consummation of the Judge's kingdom. The good news in the meantime is that we have something to work for in kingdom expectation and orientation: movement toward justice is movement away from war and violence.

What, then, does this justice look like? Old Testament scholar Bruce Waltke coined this marvelous proverb about righteousness, justice's biblical twin: "The wicked advantage themselves by disadvantaging others, but the righteous disadvantage themselves to advantage others."[1] This is as true for nations and peoples as it is for individuals. In the New Testament, we read that God's purpose for nations is not their own superiority, but the restraint of evil among their own peoples (see Romans 13:1-7). A nation that seeks its own advantage at another's expense stands in opposition to the other nation's exercise of its divine calling for the flourishing of its own people. Waltke writes that "this proverb . . . puts wisdom in shoe-leather" and "can be carried into many social situations," and this is true at the governmental and private sector level.[2]

We can see concrete examples of both successes and failures of national justice in contemporary American history. If justice entails a willingness to be disadvantaged for the other's benefit, the President's Emergency Plan for AIDS Relief (PEPFAR) is justice in action. Developed and launched by former President George W. Bush, PEPFAR devoted three billion dollars annually in a comprehensive and holistic campaign to reduce suffering from HIV/AIDS worldwide. In the overall scheme of the US budget, this isn't a huge figure. But it is still a colossal and unprecedented monetary commitment in which the American people disadvantaged themselves for the sake of other nations and peoples. I am not here arguing for the wholesale good of the PEPFAR program or that through one program a nation may be called just. Nevertheless, PEPFAR—like the Marshall Plan to which it has been compared—shows us how to recognize shadows of kingdom justice in earthly policy.

Unfortunately, examples of justice failures also abound. One notable instance is the development over the past ten years of American mechanisms for the torture and indefinite detention without trial of foreign nationals. I will not try to make the case here that "enhanced interrogation" methods like waterboarding are torture; the United States hanged Japanese soldiers for doing the same to American POWs during World War II, which seems to close the argument. Nor am I attempting to make an argument about what is or is not necessary for American national security. Instead, it is simply worth observing that by submitting non-Americans to extra-legal treatment and detention, the United States seeks its own security by disadvantaging peoples whom we imprison and abuse. And we cannot simply write off detention and abuse as a "disadvantage" that national enemies have brought on themselves. The death of combatants in war is terrible, but it is not injustice, nor is imprisonment of criminals. But by 2009, 550 Guantanamo Bay inmates, including children in their early teens, had been released without charge. This means that we have denied large numbers of people their freedom and livelihood for the sake of our own advantage, which is a denial of justice. The Christian must call such practices of detention and abuse the offenses against God's kingdom that they are.

On the broader political level, our lives are filled with both victories and failures around the prophetic vision of justice. We must surely view imbalances in resource consumption as an example of biblical injustice. Jared Diamond wrote in 2008 that people in the industrialized world consumed natural resources and generated waste at rates thirty-two times higher than those in the developing world.[3] We may not have an immediate solution, but a kingdom ethic that seeks to balance people's respective advantage over each other helps us to identify the problem.

Micah preached that benefiting from inequality led to the judgment of God, citing "dishonest scales" in commerce and the "short ephah," a measurement of dry goods. Is God "still to forget your ill-gotten treasures, you wicked house?" the prophet asks. Micah also made it clear that such gain is violence: "Your rich people are violent; your inhabitants are liars. . . . Therefore, I have begun to destroy you, to ruin you because of your sins" (Micah 6:10-12 NIV 2011).

The prophet Isaiah tells us that the shoot of Jesse—Jesus—will judge the needy with righteousness, and "with justice he will give decisions for the poor of the earth" (Isaiah 11:4). This favor for the poor and disenfranchised, which rings throughout Scripture and which Christ echoes (see Luke 6:20), is not based on the moral superiority of the materially impoverished. Being poor does not make one good. No, the reason that the poor are blessed is because they have received the bad end of the bargain in an unjust world where a few have attained their advantage at the expense of many others. But Jesus is coming back to set things right and balance the scales. Then those who have benefited from the world's fallenness—the sin profiteers—will be brought low, and those who have suffered from the same will be raised up.

Kingdom seekers should therefore seek in every way to eschew the benefits of inequality, though our efforts will be imperfect. In this spirit, we can celebrate efforts that seek systemic alleviation of global inequalities, like the fair trade movement. Land of a Thousand Hills Coffee is one shining example. Founded by an Anglican minister, Jonathan Golden, the company has established sustainable industry in Rwanda and other coffee-producing countries, paying a living wage. So we support such efforts, not because by so doing we will save the world, but because they bear the spark of a justice that rectifies imbalance. To crib from Bruce Waltke, by so doing we wrap faithfulness in shoe-leather.

INDUSTRY

In Micah's vision, we have seen that the kingdom's attributes cascade from one another, beginning with right worship of God. So justice is the preeminent virtue of peace among the nations, and it deserves the most attention. But we can also see that justice is not only an end in itself in the kingdom. It also yields the fruit of industry and nonaggression.

Standing armies were not unknown in the prophet Micah's time, but the real numbers in Israel's army came from militiamen—men making a living as farmers or tradespeople who could be called up into military service as needed by the king. In the modern West, we have professional armies to fight our wars, so many people have no immediate or even proximate experience with the horror of war. But the average family in Micah's day faced the threat of conflict breaking out and life's normalcy being interrupted. This made the cost of war a very present reality for them. The most famous line of Micah's vision—"they will beat their swords into plowshares and their spears into pruning hooks"—speaks to this context, describing a militiaman coming home from war to his farm.

The verse is often read as a generic promise of peace, but this misses its true richness. It is not about peace per se, but about the type of industry to which humans devote themselves. If the verse were just about peace, it might say, "They will lean their swords in the corner and hang their spears on the walls." Instead, we see a picture of an Israelite militiaman engaged in the creative enterprise of converting his weapons of war into agricultural instruments.

Human beings aren't static, and as we saw in the first chapter, our creative capacity mirrors the image of God. We often employ this creativity in terrible ways; the diabolic infrastructure of the Holocaust leaps to mind. But Micah foresees a day in which human creativity will be channeled toward flourishing, rather than destruction.

The primary significance of beating swords into plowshares is thus economic rather than political. In the kingdom of God, human creativity is dedicated to well-being. As we welcome this aspect of the kingdom, the question to us is how to build industries that are oriented toward this promise.

One specific ramification of kingdom movement away from industries of human destruction is on the colossal sum of money spent annually on the global military budget. Micah explicitly envisions the day not only that farmer-soldiers will return to their fields, but also that nations will not "train for war anymore."

At present, we train for war a great deal—or at least we spend like we do. Though 2010 saw the slowest annual increase in military spending since the sharp escalation following the September 11 attacks, the Stockholm International Peace Research Institute—the preeminent global authority on military spending—estimates world military expenditure that year at 1.63 trillion dollars. The United States topped the national list, with a budget of 698 billion, representing 43 percent of the global total and exceeding the combined spending of the next nine nations. China came in second, at 119 billion or 7.3 percent of the global total. Moreover, US military spending has risen 81 percent in real terms since 2001, largely due to the Iraq and Afghanistan wars, compared with a 32.5 percent aggregate increase by all other countries.[4]

Some defense expenditures will remain necessary in a fallen world. But as we have seen in Scripture, war is a consequence of injustice. We are therefore right to ask ourselves if military spending could be reduced if global injustice were reduced. We should also ask hard questions about whether such radical disparities in military spending emerge from the need to guard ourselves against the consequences of seeking our own national advantage at the expense of other peoples. In the United States, politicians from both parties treat military spending as sacred. Does a kingdom outlook suggest or permit an alternative?

The kingdom vision of human industry should also lead us into a prophetic understanding of the broader role of all business, not just the military. Christians are rightly cautious about the danger of money. Jesus cites Mammon, the god of wealth, as an exclusive competitor with God for human devotion (Matthew 6:24). The Gospel writers and Paul thoroughly condemn the love of money as "a root of all kinds of evil" (1 Timothy 6:10). And, as we saw in the previous section, God has no mercy for ill-gotten gains, for commercial enterprises that profit from exploitation.

But a rightful concern about the special peril of wealth also sometimes translates into a suspicion of business overall and an unconscious preference for nonprofit ventures. Younger Christians, especially, may view work in a nonprofit organization as more pure or kingdom-oriented than in a for-profit commercial enterprise. This is the wrong way to think.

To begin, the nonprofit's 501(c)(3) tax status is not a badge of righteousness before God. As someone who has made a career in the nonprofit arena—in both education and organizational work—I am keenly aware that my work does not generate wealth or a livelihood beyond mine, and I am humbled by the recognition that everything I do depends on the generosity of those who have created wealth and employment opportunities for others through for-profit business. This isn't to say that there's no place for nonprofits. Not everything that is good yields a material profit, making nonprofits and charities irreplaceable and worthy of support.

However, a for-profit business that can sustain its own growth, providing increased livelihood to its employees as it does so, is often a far better solution to many of the problems that nonprofits purport to solve. By no means am I intending to baptize free-market capitalism as God's own economy. Christians often give undue trust to amoral markets driven by the collective habits of wretched sinners like ourselves. But when it comes to the plummeting rates of global poverty in recent decades, empirical data seems to demonstrate that the key drivers are not small-scale activism or even foreign aid, but rather national economic growth fueled by the development of for-profit enterprise.

This should make faithful Christians committed to the development of businesses that can engage in happy commerce—*as long as they are dedicated throughout to a kingdom vision of flourishing.*

This, of course, is the catch. The capitalist system makes it easy to construct a business model that internalizes another's loss as profit— for example, competitive pricing of goods based on the low production costs of sweatshops. But alternatives do exist. In our fallen reality, no commercial enterprise will be able to operate with a perfect commitment to human flourishing—to be a purely "plowshares business." Elements of "sword business" will be present everywhere. As with every other aspect of God's kingdom, however, our inability to attain perfection should not dissuade us from orienting ourselves toward the coming reality.

Dave Kiersznowski and DEMDACO exemplify what it means to aspire toward a plowshares business. Dave is a quiet, unassuming man from Leawood, Kansas, in the dead center of America. In 1998, Dave and his wife Demi founded DEMDACO, a gift company. In Dave's words, they wholesale products that "you would expect to find in a Hallmark store."[5] DEMDACO's products are not revolutionary or hip or edgy—or any other adjective that many younger Christian activists might value. They are the sort of thing that moms and grandmothers love because they are sweet and earnest.

DEMDACO's approach to business, however, makes the company truly revolutionary in a kingdom sense. You can see this in the corporate mission statement: "We lift the spirit by restoring worth to work, helping customers succeed, promoting mutuality, and providing uplifting products." Dave and Demi have a passion to "restore *avodah*," which is a Hebrew word that they interpret in its comprehensive sense of work, worship, service and art. In Dave's own words, they are driven by a passion "to offer a different picture of business," which focuses not only on financial flourishing, but on the flourishing "of humans, of our earth, with our finances." Mutuality is key, so DEMDACO scrupulously demands that everyone involved in its business—from artist to factory to shipping to retailers to consumers—is treated justly.

The commitment to restoring worth to work is perhaps most evident at DEMDACO's own offices. It is the sort of business that upholds its community—literally from the ground up. When Dave set out to erect a building for DEMDACO headquarters, he envisioned "a place that should allow humans to flourish." The building is full of light and art, including a commissioned mural by the painter Makoto Fujimura, suggesting DEMDACO's vision of "ought, is, can, will." To remind employees that people can do good, the common areas are named after pioneers in that vein: William Wilberforce, Mother Teresa, Martin Luther King Jr. and so on.

This vision of flourishing extends beyond the physical building to the corporate ethos and practices. At DEMDACO central, hospitality is paramount, so visitors are greeted by a human being and leave with a gift. Free coffee stations and free vending machines dot the halls. It is a fun place as well. Every Wednesday at two, a vending truck rolls into the parking lot, and free ice cream is served. On Friday afternoons, employees gather in the company pub, modeled after the gathering place of C. S. Lewis and J. R. R. Tolkien's Inklings group, for a glass of wine or beer. To honor employees' minds, Dave installed an office library where people can go to read and experience quiet. Recognizing that they have bodies, he installed a workout room. Knowing that they have souls, the company goes all out on its annual Habitat for Humanity build.

Perhaps DEMDACO's most extensive and remarkable set of commitments is to the well-being of employees' families. The company has done the following:

- installed a "new mom's room" where breast milk can be pumped and stored

- built a kid-friendly "come have lunch with mom and dad" room, along with a theater that hosts regular movie nights (and popcorn fights) for employee families

- implemented a continually renewing family emergency fund, overseen by employees, to help any employee facing considerable need

- balanced the disparate costs of forming a family by childbirth (a ten-dollar copay under DEMDACO's exceptional health plan) versus adoption by offering ten thousand dollars in company money toward any employee's adoption expenses

- established a minimum employee salary that is 40 percent higher than the region's average entry-level wage

Yet perhaps the most authentic manifestation of the kingdom at DEMDACO is Dave's insistence that it is not a Christian company. Though its founders are Christians and the company's values reflect that, it is a company of people from many faiths and none, "who have bid in good conscience to come together and do good things." This speaks to the possibility of the kingdom of Christ to bless in abundance even those who do not yet recognize him as Lord.

In sum, DEMDACO appears wholly committed to the flourishing of everyone it encounters. Dave says the business's purpose is to "add to the beauty" and "to tear a little corner off the darkness," borrowing from singers Sara Groves and U2's Bono, respectively. This purpose comes out of a passionate Christian faith and a conviction that Christian ministry is not exclusively the vocation of those who work in churches.

Not every company has the financial ability to do what DEMDACO has done, of course. And though it is exceptional as a plowshares business, it is not alone in its commitments. My friend Evan Loomis comes to mind as a young entrepreneur who, like Dave, takes the idea of a kingdom-seeking business seriously. Evan and his team of founders launched TreeHouse in Austin, Texas, to be a sort of "green Home Depot"—the nation's first home- and building-supply store sourced entirely with eco-friendly products produced in socially conscious ways. The premise is genius, and by providing customers with a ready source for building with a certain ethos, TreeHouse holds as much or greater promise than any number of environmental nonprofit efforts. The company is brand-new, so its success remains to be seen. But its vision embodies the fusion of entrepreneurial spirit with the plowshares commitment to industry that builds human flourishing.

DEMDACO and TreeHouse are dramatic examples. But every instance of human activity for flourishing can be carried out with a similar kingdom mindset and exercised in ways that cause people to flourish. Imagine the revolution we would see if every Christian-owned and Christian-operated business and every Christian employee saw their work in light of such a vision.

NONAGGRESSION

The final aspect of peace among peoples is nonaggression, which is grounded in the promise that "nation will not take up sword against nation." This kingdom virtue stems from both justice and industry, since God's perfect rule of justice and the complete orientation of human creativity toward flourishing would bring all war to a halt.

In some ways, nonaggression seems the most abstract and difficult of the aspects of peace among nations. Modern international law and the UN Charter—the most widely adhered-to international agreement—already reject wars of aggression as illegal and immoral. The days of the "right of conquest," derived in part from a faulty theological assumption that all military victory signified God's blessing, are long gone. In sum, the world seems to have agreed on the principle of nonaggression, but war hasn't ceased. Is there anything left to do?

Nonaggression means far more than rejecting overt wars of territorial expansion. Nations remain actively ready to "lift up sword" against each other, and the United States is no exception. There is a deeply held American belief that all our wars are defensive, but this is simply not true. As the second Iraq War drew to a close and the final American troops left the country, historian Andrew Bacevich noted that one casualty of the conflict was

> Washington's decisive and seemingly irrevocable abandonment of any semblance of self-restraint regarding the use of violence as an instrument of statecraft. With all remaining prudential, normative, and constitutional barriers to the use of force having now been set aside, war has become a normal condition, something that the great majority of Americans accept without complaint. War is U.S.[6]

If Bacevich's diagnosis is correct, it should horrify Christians. A resignation to perpetual war is unacceptable to those who look for the kingdom of God. Nations are not meant to war with each other. Some conflict between them may be inevitable in the current fallen age, but it is not their purpose. A country whose permanent condition is war is therefore a country for which something has gone profoundly wrong. This should lead Christians into a wholesale re-evaluation of the American conception of the national interest. If "war has become a normal condition," and we desire the ability to project American power over any square inch of the globe at a moment's notice, do our ambitions not exceed the scope that God permits for a nation? Human history, which is the story of God's providence, has not been kind to those who thought to stand in God's place astride creation.

In other words, there is still plenty to do for those who welcome the kingdom promise of national nonaggression. One manifestation of nonaggression would be a widespread and substantial Christian rehabilitation of the just war tradition. This teaching, rooted in Augustine's reflections at the fall of the Roman Empire and expanded by Thomas Aquinas, has developed over fifteen centuries, yielding in the process many secular standards regarding the law of war. It stakes out areas for moral deliberation regarding the right to wage war, known as the criteria of *jus ad bellum*, and right conduct in war, or the criteria of *jus in bello*.

Unfortunately, bad interpreters of the just war tradition habitually misuse the teaching to baptize war. This gets the "just" part of "just war" entirely wrong. It is not about *justifying* war, as some talking-head TV clerics are inclined to do during times of national crisis, but rather to remind us that even the chaos of war, when we see humanity in its fullest destructive potential, is subject to the judgment and *justice* of the Prince of Peace.

This is the true gospel subversiveness of the just war tradition. We are all too ready to believe the satanic lie that war and peace are equals, peer states of being, like night and day. This is what kings and presidents, emperors and prime ministers would have us believe—for they command the forces of war. But just war declares the opposite. It shrinks war to its rightfully small portion of human life, in the tiny corner of "last resort," and even there further circumscribes the means that may be employed.

The just war tradition tells us that life is fundamentally about the pursuit of peace—in which the use of force should be but one small and infrequent tactic. If followers of the Prince of Peace wish to claim that we may have a highly circumscribed share in violence—as I would—we must accept the full discipline of the doctrine that gives us this permission: a "just war theory with teeth," as John Howard Yoder, the pacifist theologian who was one of just war's most incisive critics, often said.

What would be the fruit of such an acceptance? First, a true embrace of the just war theory aligns a believer with the kingdom promise of nonaggression. The just war tradition has a fundamental disposition *against* war, which it considers a last resort. Therefore, the believer will always be searching for an alternative to the outbreak of conflict, as well as for its earliest possible resolution. We will never welcome war as a desired goal.

Second, the just war tradition leaves the believer in an appropriately irreconcilable tension regarding ongoing armed conflict, because by its own standards a "just war" is virtually impossible. World War II is often cited as an example of a just war, given the gravity of the Allied cause and the evil of Axis aggression. By the time of its outbreak, it may indeed have been a war that had to be fought. But it was not a just war, because it was not prosecuted as such. This is not to say the two sides were morally equivalent, but the Allies also failed to protect enemy noncombatant lives and to use proportionate means.

A just war sensibility prevents the Christian from ever becoming a cheerleader for war, which is an untenable position for anyone who embraces the coming kingdom. In our present circumstances, the just war tradition can lead to profound discomfort with policies like the reliance on drone warfare, for example, in which it is extremely difficult to distinguish between combatant and innocent, and which has killed hundreds of Afghani and Pakistani civilians, including many children.[7]

Third, a robust understanding of just war carries the implicit requirement to work actively for peace. Just war is a tradition grounded in nonaggression. If justice and the rule of law are absent and if human industry degrades dignity and destroys flourishing, a war of last resort may still be quite near. But where a commitment to justice and human flourishing abounds between nations, the last resort of war may be so distant as to be unimaginable—as is the case between the United States and the United Kingdom, for example.

In Washington, DC, as in capitals around the world, those who are willing to declare their allegiance to peace are often called naïve and foolish by worldly pragmatists. But it is the supposed pragmatists who are naïve. They only see the world right before their eyes and act with corresponding realism. Kingdom-minded peacemakers, however, are the ultimate pragmatists, for we know that our vindication is as final and sure as the sovereign victory of our Lord.

9

PEACE IN COMMUNITY

Dignity, Prosperity, Security

Every man will sit under his own vine
and under his own fig tree,
and no one will make them afraid,
for the LORD *Almighty has spoken.*

MICAH 4:4

PERCIVAL GEORGE RHODA, PhD

Paarl is named for the oddly domed stone hill that looms over the city, because the Dutch settlers thought it gleamed in the rain like a pearl. But as my wife and I approach the city in the brilliant November morning sun—late spring in South Africa—it just looks like a big gray rock. I can feel Natalie's tension as she sits next to me in the passenger seat of our rental car. She has known this day would come for almost a year, and has been waiting her entire life. She is terrified of being disappointed and is preparing to be underwhelmed.

Natalie has been steeling herself all week. When she landed in Cape Town last Tuesday, she became the first member of her immediate family to set foot in South Africa, her ancestral homeland on her mother's side, in over four decades. She wasn't expecting an electric shock to run through the soles of her feet the first time she stepped on African soil, but she has been surprised at how foreign the place feels. It does not feel like she has found a long-lost home.

This makes a certain sense, though it saddens too. Her grandparents and their three children fled the country for England in 1966. The youngest child, Chantal, was ten years old, and none of them ever went back. Chantal grew to adulthood by the mouth of the Thames, married Andy, a red-haired Essex boy, and Natalie arrived in due time.

For Natalie, South Africa existed only in corporeal traces and family legacies: her own olive skin and dark, curly hair; her mother's cappuccino complexion; her maternal grandmother's exotic, clipped accent; some pictures of the family home they had left; a few family stories; and old wives' tales that were clearly not English in origin—like her grandmother's insistence that an open nursery window was an invitation for snakes to sneak in and eat Natalie's little sister, Danielle.

Perhaps one trace rose above them all: the memories of her remarkable grandfather, Percival George Rhoda, PhD, a man who died only two years after bringing his family to England, yet lived on in the adoring memory of his wife and daughter.

But even these traces faded. When Chantal and Andy immigrated to Canada in the hopes of a better life for their daughters, South Africa faded even further into memory. There lay wells of trauma and sorrow, Natalie and her sister knew, and so it was rarely discussed.

Natalie longed to know more of her family's history and homeland, however. So the day we discovered that I would attend the Cape Town 2010 Lausanne Congress on World Evangelization was the day we began planning Natalie's first trip to her ancestral home. A year later, I flew in for the Congress, and she arrived a few days after to do theological research and interviews with local communities about the post-apartheid Truth and Reconciliation Commission.

Now, with the Congress over, we are spending several days in the spectacular Cape Winelands. On our first day, we drive into Paarl, the city from which my wife's family fled nearly five decades earlier, on a mission to find traces of the grandfather she never met.

We are armed with precious little information. We have a street name and house number. Natalie's recollection of a faded photograph of the family home, showing distinctive stonework fronting the building. Chantal's memory of the view from the stoop, with green vineyards directly across the street and soaring mountains beyond. Noorder-Paarl Secondary, the name of the Colored high school where Dr. Rhoda served as principal and Mrs. Rhoda taught needlepoint. And the knowledge of why they left: that the mixture of apartheid's tightening grip and Dr. Rhoda's increasing political activity had begun to put the family in danger. With such few leads, we are prepared for the day to be a bust.

Instead, the hours that follow unfold as if scripted by a benevolent author, though we can't see this at first. The GPS lays out a course that mirrors Chantal's memory. We begin by turning from School Street's long stretch onto Reitz Street, where a line of neat homes fronts an expanse of vine rows and the Hawequas Mountains rising in the east. The only problem is the house numbering—we are looking for number 4, which does not exist. Several homes have the stonework recollected from the old photograph. Perhaps the street has been expanded and the lots renumbered? Does the house still exist? We explain our situation to a man watering his front garden, and he helpfully directs us to the municipal planning authority: "Corner of Market and Main, third floor—but they'll be closed this morning."

With some time to kill, we find our way to Noorder-Paarl Secondary, which is an imposing white-columned building fronted by a large lawn. It occurs to us that our story sounds dubious: a young woman of ambiguous ethnicity with a foreign accent in a nation where skin and voice still mean a great deal, arriving without warning with a white American husband in tow, claiming that her grandfather was principal of this school nearly a half century ago—and she is wanting what, exactly?

As Natalie begins to explain herself to the mildly flummoxed and visibly skeptical school secretary, I wander around the lobby looking at the trophies, banners and photos on display. And then, there they are: Dr. and Mrs. Rhoda, unmistakable in a photo of school faculty, dated 1961. Adrenaline tightens my throat.

"Natalie!" I hiss. "Natalie!" She dashes over, and sees, and tears flood her eyes to find the image of the grandfather she never knew and the grandmother she loved, hanging there on the wall of a school halfway around the planet from any home she has ever known. And the receptionist, a sudden convert to our cause, is overwhelmed as well and is sticking her head into neighboring offices and the hallway, calling this and that passing faculty member over to see, look, this is the granddaughter of Dr. and Mrs. Rhoda, who taught here so long ago—see the picture!—and she has come to see us, she has come home.

Within minutes a teacher has whisked us into a school tour, speeding through the hallways and crowds of students, whose bright faces follow us curiously, intrigued by such obviously foreign visitors. "One of the teachers in that photo of your grandparents is still alive," he tells us. "Would you like to visit him?"

So, after some hasty record checking and phone calling on our behalf, we find ourselves driving to see Mr. Davids in Wellington, the adjacent town, where Natalie's grandmother was born. The dapper young teacher in the neat suit and tie is now an old man, retired and bedridden from recent illness, but he and his family receive us warmly. "Your grandfather was no respecter of persons," he tells Natalie. "I remember the White school superintendent walked straight into his office unannounced, and your grandfather looked right at him and asked him if he had an appointment. Made him go away and come back the next day!" Decades later, the episode still makes him chortle, laughter shaking his old bones.

Later that afternoon, we arrive at the municipal authority, and Natalie tells her now-familiar story to two desk clerks, explaining our question about the house number. After a rapid-fire exchange in Afrikaans, they both vanish into the back office. Minutes later, a head pokes around the corner: "Your grandfather's name was Rhoda, yes?" The pair emerges with a large green land deed. There, the first owner, P. G. Rhoda. Next to his name, the column labeled "Owner/ Race," marked "C" for Colored, an indelible memorial to the brazen prejudice of a bygone regime.

They pull out survey maps, correlate the deed with the property and pull it up on Google Maps, angling the monitor so we can see. "Here is your grandparents' home," they say, pointing to a green-roofed house at the corner of Reitz Street and Martin Street. As we leave, they hand us color photocopies of the deed and the map, smiling.

Fifteen minutes later, we are back where we started our day. There it is—number 16, in fact—the house that her grandfather built, a tidy, well-kept home, low slung and white walled like so many houses in this Mediterranean climate, with a pretty front yard. A knock on the door elicits no response, and we are a bit relieved not to meet those who have inherited, even indirectly, from the Rhoda family's loss. Then, sitting on the curb in the warm afternoon sun, Natalie calls her mother in Canada. "Mummy, I'm here at your old house. Yes. Yes, Reitz Street. Yes, the stone and the vineyards. It's beautiful. Yes. . . . Yes. . . . Yes."

We leave Paarl buoyant, cross a bridge over the Berg River and drive toward the mountains lit by the reddening dusk. We arrived hours ago with modest hopes of glimpsing the terrain from which Natalie's family had come. We are departing, instead, with a land-scape portrait. And upon our return to North America, our stories and photographs will unlock previously unheard family stories, re-vealing the cartography of a man who sought the peace of his com-munity in an era that offered no peace.

THE PARADISE OF ORDINARY PLEASURES

Today's South Africa is a new country. For university students, Nelson Mandela and Desmond Tutu are living history—but history nonetheless. As the country looks to a twenty-first-century Africa, it is anxious to be done with the legacy of the most viciously sys-tematic racial segregation and oppression in modern times.

In that day, the country was divided into White, Black and Colored. The latter designation was given both to lighter-skinned Africans and to mixed-race individuals—the Rhodas were both. Their family tree included both the warm-skinned Khoi tribe, known colonially as Hottentots, as well as French Huguenot missionaries and Scottish immigrants. Coloreds occupied an insecure middle mi-nority during apartheid, neither accepted nor entirely rejected by the diametrically opposed European Whites and African Blacks. The legacy of this in-between status still lingers today, one of the many ways that even a visitor can feel apartheid's traces.

Micah's Israel evidences the same diabolic collapse of peace in community. Unlike apartheid, the details of this oppression's impact on ordinary Israelites at the time are lost to history and Scripture's spare narrative. But we can discern its shape from the prophets who called down the kingdom of God against it.

Micah and Isaiah prophesied in an era when the Israelite way of life teetered on the brink. Both the northern kingdom of Israel and the southern kingdom of Judah had endured generations of kings who were mostly indifferent to the law and its prohibition of injustice and earthly militarism. Old Testament scholar Chris Wright writes that a rising class of wealthy and exploitive tradesmen acquired family farms and aggregated them into large land holdings, turning individual farmers into tenant laborers. According to Wright, this development profoundly threatened the "network of free, landowning families" that formed the foundation of the covenant society, given the family unit's place at the center of a triangle linked to the nation of Israel, the land and God.[1]

Because this dispossession at the hands of wealthy landowners endangered the very productivity that made Israel a promised land, it provoked the wrath of God: "Woe to you who add house to house and join field to field till no space is left and you live alone in the land" (Isaiah 5:8). Therefore, Isaiah says, ten acres of vines will produce barely six gallons of wine, and 360 pounds of seed will yield only a tenth of their weight in grain—a death sentence for an agricultural society. The aggressive Assyrian Empire stood at Israel's doorstep, injustice and immorality reigned among the rich and powerful in Jerusalem, and the common people found themselves evicted from their ancestral land. This was an existential threat.

Micah's vision of the coming kingdom was basic, because the prophet saw that heaven's joys are not complex: one day, everyone would sit under their own vine and their own fig tree, and no one would make them afraid. In other words, peace in community would be restored. Micah's promise would have sounded like the paradise of everyday life, in the way that hardship like illness or unemployment makes us long for the simplest pleasures, like health and work.

The deprivation of Percival Rhoda's South Africa was both similar and different. By virtue of the parents' education and profession, the Rhoda family lived an exceptional existence—materially comfortable and thoroughly upper-middle class. They did not want, though many around them did. Yet they still suffered from a comprehensive denial of the peace in community that Micah foresaw.

The apartheid system was a political undertaking by a fearful White minority to ensure their dominance among the Black and Colored majority in a country that their ancestors had colonized and conquered. The Whites were afraid of what would happen to them if all South Africans were equal—a fear that may not have been unwarranted, given their manifold sins and those of their forebears. Apartheid attempted to ensure the human dignity, prosperity and security of Whites by systematically denying the same for Blacks and Coloreds.

For this reason, it was doomed from the start, though this was far from obvious at its height. Peace in community cannot be hoarded by only one portion of the population. It does not exist unless it is shared by all. Impressions to the contrary are willful delusions, like those of the court prophets in Jeremiah's day, who said, "'Peace, peace' . . . when there is no peace" (Jeremiah 6:14). Oppression can suppress violence, but it cannot bring about peace.

We have seen that Micah has a linear vision of the peaceable kingdom. Every aspect proceeds from the one that precedes it. For example, peace among the nations emerges from peace with God, and industry and nonaggression depend on justice. The third cluster—peace in community—is harder to parse because its attributes occur simultaneously. *Dignity, prosperity* and *security* dance together, a perichoresis of earthly peace. Where dignity is, there too is prosperity and security. Remove either of the latter, and all collapse. But all three together reveal this peace in the way that every side of a well-cut jewel sparkles in the flat plane of a single facet. Because of this interdependence, peace in community can be described only through the complex narratives of real lives.

DIGNITY

A frenetic scene unfolds on the road marking the vineyard's western border. A Black man hurtles down the street in a headlong sprint. A White man on a horse gallops after him, holding the reins in one hand. In the other, he awkwardly balances an unwieldy rifle, with which he is taking errant shots at the running man. It is 1960.

It is hard to shoot straight from a moving horse, and the shots are going wild. But a man with a gun on a horse chasing an unarmed man on foot across open ground is a story that has only one ending.

Unless, that is, another man leaps from the garden he has been tending, into the road between the charging horse and running man, and yells, "Stop, stop!"

Now the story has changed. The White man with the rifle on the horse is the vineyard foreman. The panting Black man—we don't know who he is yet. And the man who has burst into the street is Mr. Rhoda, not yet in possession of his PhD. The vineyard foreman knows him. Mr. Rhoda is Colored, yes, but he is a principal at a nearby secondary school, a respected man in the community and, against all racial convention, an acquaintance of the White farmer who owns the vineyard. Every Sunday after church, the farmer wanders across his vine rows to Mr. Rhoda's home, where Mr. Rhoda receives him with a glass of sherry and conversation about the affairs of the day. They are not friends, precisely, but there is mutual respect there. In other words, the mounted man with the gun is now standing before someone who must be recognized.

"What's going on here?" Mr. Rhoda demands.

"This man was stealing," the foreman replies. "He was digging among the harvest gleanings for grapes." Mr. Rhoda looks at the Black man and knows that this is true. He appears to be far from home—certainly some inland village. He is obviously desperate, and his situation is about to be made much worse by his being shot dead in the middle of Reitz Street.

"That's impossible," Mr. Rhoda says, feigning a note of outrage. "He works for me. He couldn't have been stealing."

The lie is ridiculous, and all three know it. The vineyard foreman knows Mr. Rhoda does not employ this man, knows that he has probably never seen this man. Mr. Rhoda knows it, of course. And the Black man definitely knows it. But a lie that will save a man's life is truth itself when held up against the legislated lie that gives a White man the right to shoot a Black man for pilfering discarded grapes. Somehow the legislated lie seemed believable in the dusky halls of power to the soft-faced men who wrote it into being. But there are no shadows here. The sun blazes down on the men on the road and on their dueling lies, and it pronounces its incorruptible verdict.

The foreman stares at Mr. Rhoda and at Mr. Rhoda's new employee. Then he wheels his horse and rides away, leaving the pair alone in the sun and the dust.

"What's your name?" Mr. Rhoda asks the man.

"Klaas," he replies.

*Every*one and every *one* will sit under their own vine, Micah promises. It is a perfect balance of the community and the individual, in which both serve the welfare of the other. For Micah, the one sitting under the vine is not an isolated individual; rather, he serves as a literary stand-in for a thriving family unit, for whom agricultural bounty is the cornerstone of existence. At the same time, neither the individual nor the family is an isolated island, because all will be similarly blessed—an archipelago of abundance.

Such questions of individual rights versus community good are relevant to contemporary contexts as well. It is easy to tip the balance too far in one direction or the other, crushing the individual for the perceived need of the community or allowing the individual to excel at the community's expense. But Micah's vision errs in neither direction; it portrays a society of perfect human dignity.

Percival Rhoda lived out a remarkable commitment to this balance by perceiving the universal in the particular. A man fleeing down the street is a *man* and therefore worth saving, no matter who he is or isn't. And yet it is never *man* writ large who must be saved— some concept or ideal that lives in the petri dish of ideology—but *this* man, soon to be known as Klaas, whom God has placed on this road at this time and thus entrusted to Mr. Rhoda's care.

Klaas moved in that day. The next Sunday, when the vineyard owner came for his sherry, there was Klaas, his labor a happy proof that he could not have stolen any grapes. To contemporary Westerners, a live-in servant may seem the exclusive province of the hyper-wealthy, but in many contexts around the world, such arrangements were (and still are) common even for the middle class, through which economic prosperity was extended to those who otherwise might have lived in destitution. Mr. Rhoda built a small addition onto the house so Klaas could have his own apartment, and Klaas worked for the family until they left the country years later.

Twice a year the entire family would pack into the car for the twelve-hour round-trip journey to Klaas's village—first to drop him off for his vacation and a month later to pick him back up. When they arrived to retrieve him, Klaas would be waiting with his suitcase by the road, ready to return from his family's straw dwellings to the suburban life he had come to enjoy. But his family always insisted on receiving the Rhodas and extending hospitality, so they would go into the low huts to eat and talk. In the slanted memory of childhood, my mother-in-law recalls every drive as a single, long lecture from her father about the manners they were to display for the visit: they were to eat and drink anything that was offered to them, no matter how unfamiliar. They were to sit in a hut in their neat, pressed clothing and converse politely as though it were their daily habit. They were to treat Klaas's relatives just as they would the king and queen of England.

Such manners were a dominant theme in the Rhoda household, but not for putting on airs. Rather, Dr. and Mrs. Rhoda raised their children to be able to talk to anyone, no matter their social status. The point was to stand readily on the level of whomever they encountered—to meet people of high station or low with the dignity afforded a human being.

In Paarl in the early 1960s, manners that recognized a universal dignity could be a revolutionary act. Consider the context and the regard usually shown to non-Whites. A few years after Klaas arrived on the scene, two Black boys went missing in the Hawequas Mountains outside of Paarl. The area was known as a haunt for disreputable teenagers to smoke dope and drink, but these were errant children, no more than ten or eleven years old. The White police were called in and eventually found the boys, alive but only just. They had fallen into a steep ravine, a cleft in the mountain. The police deemed the location impassable and said there was no way for a man safely to descend into the narrow crack, secure the two boys and ascend again with both their weight.

Instead, the police proposed that the boys be shot. They were visible where they lay. They were suffering from dehydration. It was the decent thing to do, the police said, just as one would do for a lost animal—a sheep, say, fallen beyond the ability to rescue—which required putting down.

Dr. Rhoda and his colleagues stepped in. They thanked the police for finding the boys, declined the suggestion for next steps and sent them home. Then they organized the rescue party, raised the money and coordinated the retrieval, which proved not to be very difficult at all.

Around that time, on the Rhoda family's annual sojourn to pick up Klaas from his vacation, they saw beside the road a man who had been burned to death and hung high in a tree. Around his feet gathered a gaggle of African children, staring at the terrible bough above them. Dr. Rhoda pulled over and ordered his family to stay in the car. He walked over and looked at the body. He knelt and spoke with the children. They ran off and presently returned with a group of men from a nearby village, whom Dr. Rhoda organized into a party to bring the body down and bury it. Then he got back in the car and the family proceeded to Klaas's village.

I interrupt my mother-in-law's telling of the story. "Why do you think your father stopped?"

She is shocked by the question. "Of course he stopped," she says. "Anyone would have."

But, of course, this is not true. Not everyone in 1960s South Africa stops on a rural road to arrange the burial of a burned Black body found hanging from a tree. A lynching serves as a warning against getting involved. There are many who simply avert their eyes and drive on. I point out to my mother-in-law that this is not just my subjective opinion but the fact of this particular case: if the body had been hanging there long enough for the perpetrators to leave and for a child then to find it and to gather his friends, then certainly others on the road had seen the body and left their foot steady on the accelerator.

She is unconvinced. "I don't know. It wasn't dignified," she says, with finality, and that settles it. Dignity is its own proof.

PROSPERITY

My mother-in-law was born on Christmas Day, and her father decided that with his wife otherwise occupied, he would teach himself how to cook. Later that evening, he laid out the Christmas dinner, a feast of turkey, roast potatoes, carrots, parsnips and gravy. Delighted with his accomplishment, Mr. Rhoda resolved that Christmas dinner would thereafter be his domain, and every year he reprised his role in the kitchen, to the bemusement of his wife and children.

Years later, after the family moved to England, one morning Mrs. Rhoda came downstairs to hear music from the piano, at which she was well versed. There sat her husband, who had never received musical training, sounding out a serviceable and evidently improving tune.

Another time, he taught himself Russian.

Such autodidactic episodes help explain a life that is otherwise baffling. Percival Rhoda—born in 1912, somewhere in the middle of eight siblings, to Jacob and Mary Rhoda, late of Elsie's River, Cape Town—was not supposed to get an education, let alone a doctorate from the Sorbonne in Paris. Instead, he was supposed to do as his brothers did, leaving school as soon as he was old enough to help his father lay bricks. For some reason that nobody knows, he didn't leave school early, or at the end of his secondary education, or even after completing his university degree. Dr. Rhoda's diploma from the Sorbonne hangs today in my mother-in-law's home, itself a tacit example of the possibilities of his dissertation's subject: "A Survey of Education in South Africa with Special Reference to the Coloured People or more specifically a Survey of Coloured Education in South Africa."

His lived-out faith in education proved definitive for his identity: in the way he and his wife raised their children, in his professional vocation as a principal and in the focus of the political work that would eventually force the Rhodas to leave South Africa. For Dr. Rhoda, education contained the possibility of prosperity for an entire community.

Micah resonates with this impulse in his promise that the Israelites would sit under their own vines and their own fig trees. It, too, is a promise of comprehensive prosperity. *Prosperity* has become a loaded term, given the rise of the unbiblical "prosperity gospel," but the excesses of that non-gospel could not be further from the simple virtues marking Micah's vision of the good life. For Micah, prosperity is the freedom to flourish.

This begins with a freedom from unjust oppression. For the Israelites whose family lands had been taken away and who were forced to work the fields of another, the hope of resting under the fruits of their own labor meant the possibility of not having their work serve another's gain. It was such a tempting promise that the king of Assyria, besieger of Jerusalem, tried to employ it for the sake of an easy surrender. Your God cannot secure you, he said. Instead, "make peace with me and come out to me. Then every one of you will eat fruit from your own vine and fig tree . . . until I come and take you to a land like your own" (Isaiah 36:16-17 NIV 2011). But the pledge of working under any rule but God's is a lie for a people who wish to be free.

This was the promise of teaching South Africa's non-White children. Apartheid systematically denied Coloreds and Blacks the same rights of self-determination that were given to Whites. The only possible way out was education. For Dr. Rhoda, achieving a level of education sufficient to help train his community meant intensive amounts of travel outside the country, given the restricted opportunities available within South Africa's borders. Armed with expertise gleaned abroad, a network of overseas contacts and a position as a principal, he was then able to implement a vision of a day when Colored and Black students would reap the benefit of their own learning—rather than simply having their industry bolster the covetousness of a ruling minority.

Chantal recalls education as the warp and woof of their family. Every aspect of the Rhodas's daily life had an educational component, perhaps to a fault. Vacations revolved around museums, historic sites and lessons in history. The Rhodas sent away for mail-order exercises to supplement their children's normal school lessons, leading to late-night sessions learning mathematics at the kitchen table. Chantal received a special book with a weekly list of words; every Friday, she and her father had conversations in which she employed her newly expanded vocabulary. In their regular evening devotionals, Dr. Rhoda read long sections from the Bible and asked the children what they thought about them. He extended a similar concern to his many nieces and nephews, taking special care to mentor them, as the sole family member to have attended college.

This educational commitment was paired with Percival Rhoda's extraordinary work ethic. The work of learning and educating those in his care, from his family to the Noorder-Paarl Secondary students who passed through his office, occupied most of his attention. Yet his side projects evidenced an astoundingly diverse and comprehensive vision for his community, many of which he executed with a group of friends. They met under the cover of the Masons, which provided a way around apartheid's increasingly severe restrictions on the ability of non-Whites to congregate and travel. Journeying as Masons visiting their brethren in other lodges, Dr. Rhoda and a handful of friends regularly traveled the country, talking with educators and financial institutions about concrete ways to raise the quality of life for Coloreds and Blacks.

They spoke from experience, having raised funds to establish the first non-White building society in Paarl, which offered horizon-expanding loan capital for new construction. And, because life is not only labor, they also bought a building and set up a cinema so that Coloreds and Blacks could enjoy a night out at the movies—a pleasure otherwise denied them by the Whites-only cinema. The latter project seems in keeping with a man whose personal sternness was leavened by an abundant sense of fun, which took such forms as regular family bike rides, an insatiable love for chocolate and a fondness for wagering on the ponies.

The simple values of work and the rhythm of rest are built into this understanding of prosperity. When many people think of what prosperity means, they imagine decadent luxury. Such a life was imaginable to the Israelites in Micah's day. The oppression of the wealthy landowners led to wealth and "great houses" and "fine mansions," the destruction of which Isaiah foretold (Isaiah 5:9). But kingdom prosperity is not life lived at levels allowed by such ill-gotten gains, nor is it a life of relaxation. Sitting under one's own vine does not imply the pleasures of vacation, but rather the satisfaction at the end of a day's work. It is easy to forget that work was created good and that we experience it as toil only because of the fall. We were made to work and to flourish in our labor, and Micah sees a heaven that both bustles with activity and enjoys the rhythm of rest.

Of course, Coloreds and Blacks could neither educate nor work themselves into the privileges of another skin. That was one of apartheid's singular cruelties: the more one learned and strove, the more one became conscious of the invisible bars that imprisoned the majority of the population.

I asked Chantal what adjectives she would use to describe her father. She paused for a moment and said, "Speaking as an adult, I can see he was frustrated and angry. And yet he also had an almost childlike excitement at the possibility that everything could be better than it was." This pairing makes sense. A proud and perpetually optimistic man living under a political system whose express purpose was the denial of hope would indeed be frustrated and angry.

She did not describe her father as cynical, however, and this makes all the difference. I imagine that it would have been exceptionally easy for Dr. Rhoda to become bitter and to retreat entirely from any effort to boost his community's prosperity—knowing that every gain would be paired with frustration at how great it could have been without apartheid's shackles. Yet he continued, seemingly with every breath, not because his work and education would defeat apartheid—though perhaps he believed it could—but because the very act of working in spite of it testified to the existence of another, unseen world. Karl Barth's description of the gospel comes to mind:

> We have therefore, in the power of God, a look-out, a door, a hope; and even in this world we have the possibility of following the narrow path and of taking each simple little step with a "despair which has its own consolation" (Luther). The prisoner becomes a watchman. Bound to his post as firmly as a prisoner in his cell, he watches for the dawning of the day.[2]

Dr. Rhoda knew what not everyone in Paarl knew: there was a bigger world beyond 1960s South Africa. And in this reality—somewhere, somehow, someday—his community could prosper. So, though his learning and his work only made him angrier at the prison they increasingly revealed, they also allowed him and, to an extent, those whose lives he touched to stand in their cells as citizens of a world in which they were free.

SECURITY

In 1960, a Whites-only national referendum voted to make South Africa a republic. This distanced South Africa from the British Commonwealth, which was increasingly hostile to the apartheid government, and began a hardening of apartheid policies domestically. The Republic of South Africa formed on May 31, 1961, and commemorated the date as Republic Day. To celebrate, every year the government sent a box of little flags to South African schools. The flags were distributed to the children, who were then to wave them about on Republic Day to show their patriotic love for the apartheid government.

Dr. Rhoda took Noorder-Paarl Secondary's box of Republic Day flags home and burned it in the yard.

He did not undertake this action in secret. In fact, he made a small ceremony out of it, which would have been readily visible from both Martin Street and Reitz Street. On one level, he simply refused to enable and preside over a day that commemorated his community's increased oppression. From the apartheid government's perspective, this was probably bad enough for a public educator. But in publicly declaring his unwillingness to be coopted, he made a much deeper refusal as well, which cuts to the heart of every authoritarian regime ever devised by humankind: he refused to fear.

The final promise of Micah's vision, and the third aspect of peace in community, anchors his vision in *security*: "and no one will make them afraid." Fear was routine in Micah's Israel. Psalm 10 could describe the time well: "In his arrogance the wicked man hunts down the weak. . . . His victims are crushed, they collapse. . . . He says to himself, 'God has forgotten; he covers his face and never sees'" (Psalm 10:2, 10-11). The wealthy could do as they pleased with the lives of ordinary people, who had no recourse in the face of forces beyond their control. In truth, this has been the condition for normal people in most parts of the world for the vast majority of human history. Fear is the favorite weapon of every earthly principality, which is precisely why the Bible's consistent witness to the alternative, the kingdom of God, is so punctuated with injunctions for the faithful to "fear not."

This is more than a promise that someday we will not be afraid anymore. That promise of future fearlessness, for those who receive it in faith, means that there is nothing to fear *now*. It is fitting for a prophetic kingdom vision that begins with worshipful fear of God to end with fearlessness of all humankind.

One afternoon in the early 1960s, Dr. Rhoda is at a meeting at the

Masonic lodge, conspiring about how to improve the lives of Coloreds and Blacks. His wife decides to drive over and give him a ride
home. Eight-year-old Chantal tags along, always eager for a chance
to be around her father. When they arrive, he is saying good-bye to
his friends. Is he surprised to see his wife? Perhaps. He thanks her
for coming, but as it is a warm evening, he has been looking forward
to a pleasant walk home. Does she mind?

No, of course she doesn't. But—and here she looks sternly at
him—he is not to walk across *that* bridge. They both know what she
is talking about: between the lodge and the Rhodas' home runs the
Berg River, and the most direct route across it goes through a beautiful riverfront park that Paarl residents frequently use for picnics,
outings and baptisms. In recent months, however, a group of Whites
has decided that they do not want to share such a nice spot, and so
they have embarked on an extralegal campaign to violently harass
and threaten any non-Whites who dare to come near. It has become
unsafe. Mrs. Rhoda knows her husband is not a man to let others
determine where he can and cannot walk, and so he may need a reminder about avoiding the area.

At the same time that Mrs. Rhoda is laying down the law, Chantal
has erupted into a squeaky explosion: "Can I go with Daddy can I
please go with Daddy Daddy please can I walk with you?" He smiles
and nods and says of course. Perhaps his wife assumes that he is
agreeing to both of them: of course Chantal may walk with him and
of course he will find a detour around that park.

So Dr. Rhoda and Chantal set off together, and Mrs. Rhoda
drives home.

The evening is beautiful, and the father and daughter enjoy walking
and talking and laughing with each other. He relishes time with his
beloved youngest child, and she is giddy to have the exclusive attention of the father she adores. Distracted with delight, she does not

notice his mood slowly begin to shift. She misses his increasing attention on the path in front of them, the distracted edge that creeps into his voice, as they walk straight toward the very bridge that he is under strict matrimonial orders to avoid at all costs. She is laughing and giggling until the path opens up onto the bridge in front of them, and she suddenly realizes that they are not simply out for a stroll.

Dr. Rhoda is deadly serious now, silent, as the two arrive at the foot of the bridge spanning the Berg, which means "Mountain River" in Afrikaans. They pause and look together across its span, to the group of White men standing on the other side, who have also gone quiet and are staring back. The space between them thrums like a severed nerve. The daughter looks to her father, and the fear on her face asks the question: what are they to do? They could turn around and walk away. Perhaps something in him wishes to do so, to spare her this trial. Perhaps it takes everything in him not to pick her up in his arms and run, run, run.

But Dr. Rhoda so loves his daughter that he does not run. Instead, he bends down and opens his heavy bag, which contains the Masonic lodge's assorted paraphernalia. He pulls out a golden chain and wraps it tightly around his knuckles. Then he takes his bag in the other hand, looks down at his daughter, and they step onto the bridge. Though she is terrified by the legion of hatred on the other side, she must follow. She remembers it vividly even today, across the nearly half century: her fingers' desperate ache to hold her father's hand. But she cannot, because he is holding his bag. So, left with no alternative than courage, she walks bravely next to him, arms swinging purposefully at her sides.

The White men have begun to yell obscenities now, which grow louder and more explicit and vicious as Dr. Rhoda and Chantal make their way toward them. The men stand in a roiling cluster, feeding off each other's venom, heaving and pulsing with threat, like a jellyfish. Chantal is crying, but she understands that they are to be silent, so she does not speak. Her gaze flits between the men, electric in their vitriol, and her father, whose face now burns.

This father is not a man with illusions. He knows that his little girl will grow up in a hard and brutal place. He knows that this will not be the last bridge she must ever cross, and others may be guarded by yowling demons even worse than these. And he knows, in a way that a child cannot, that he will not always be with her to hold her hand.

He is so filled with love for her that his face is dead with hate. Not hate for the men that oppose them, for they are only men. No, hate for the demon that so robs grown men of decency that they will scream at a little girl; hate for the fear she is made to feel; hate for the world and its many bridges that will cause his child to cry; hate for the cruelty of knowing that someday she must cross bridges alone.

They cross the bridge and pass the shouting, spitting men, and they make their way home. There her mother discovers what has transpired and raises the holiest of all hells.

Chantal remembers feeling proud of him at the time, albeit terrified. She also remembers revisiting the memory with horror after having young children of her own, long after her father had died: she could not imagine taking Natalie or Danielle through a similar ordeal. I ask her what she thinks today. "I could never put them through that, but I didn't have to raise them in that world. I'm glad that I went through it," she says. "I think it made me a stronger person."

I ask her whether crossing the bridge made her less afraid, after. She doesn't hesitate: "Oh, yes."

There it is: he was teaching her not to fear. The story can be nothing but this. We know that the bridge and its crossing are not an accident, an event that befalls him, a happenstance of which he is a victim. But we would be wrong to think that the event indicates some lack of concern for his daughter. Quite the opposite. She is the baby of the family, his favorite. Their time together, telling stories and laughing, is the delight of his life. He does not bring her to the bridge to do her harm. He brings her to the bridge because he loves her more than he loves anything in this world, and his beloved child must survive the wearing of dark skin in apartheid South Africa. He is not taking her into danger. No, he is taking his daughter on a walk on a beautiful evening, and the world in which they walk is dangerous. There is a difference.

A man and his child, whom he loves, come to the Mountain River. There he stoops to bind himself with a chain of gold, that his child might walk free. Stop. Listen. We have heard this story elsewhere—other fathers, other children, other bindings, other emancipations.

Does he destroy every demon that faces them? No, he does not even strike out at them with the chain that wraps his hand. But with it he will fetter the fear that turns women and men away from bridges in the first place. He will teach his daughter that there is nothing truly to fear, in the only way that such teaching can be taught. He will rip at the darkness in the hope of giving her a glimpse of the day to come, when the wicked will "terrify no more" (Psalm 10:18), and the night of fear will evaporate with the light of love.

FOR THE LORD ALMIGHTY HAS SPOKEN

Dignity, prosperity and security. We can find the three aspects of peace in every human community to various degrees, where they fertilize the soil in which our most intimate, quotidian joys take root and sprout. When we have these three in abundance, even life's unavoidable losses can carry a redeemed nobility—think of the death of a family elder at the end of a long life, surrounded by flourishing children and grandchildren. Against starkly barren landscapes like apartheid South Africa, however, the green shoots of peace are all the more striking—and fragile.

Most of us have little control over the climate in which we live. It may be lush and green, allowing peace to spring up like weeds in springtime. Or it might be fickle and dry, with intermittent rain and frangible soil. That part isn't up to us. But we can resolve to be gardeners no matter what the weather brings. When Martin Luther was asked what he would do if he knew the world would end tomorrow, he famously replied that he would plant an apple tree today.

The operative value here is the conviction that God is a bringer of growth in one form or another. This is why we don't have to be the hero of the story, just the steward of our calling. Peace in community is going to happen. It won't be complete until the last days, yes, but it's a done deal. So, even if our times seem bleak, we can still sow the seeds of dignity, prosperity and security with confidence in every community plot to which we have access.

The trick is thoroughness. If we cultivate this peace in how we regard others, we can then seed small plots, like our individual friendships and immediate families, which leads to the pollination of larger and larger fields, like churches, neighborhoods and cities.

Some of us struggle to believe in the promise of such peace. It can be difficult to believe that anything like it could ever bloom in the desert terrain of our relationships. It can seem easier simply to acclimate to the landscape around us, growing hard and arid and cracked until nothing differentiates us from the dead soil on which we stand. That's understandable but finally tragic, because peace is coming.

How do we know? Because *the Lord Almighty has spoken*. When a drought plagued ancient Israel, Elijah prayed for rain on Mount Carmel. Seven times he put his face between his knees and sent his servant to look toward the sea. Six times his servant reported a sky dry and dead as cement. But the seventh time, he returned and told the prophet, "A cloud as small as a man's hand is rising from the sea" (1 Kings 18:44).

So Elijah got up, gathered his robe into his belt, and in the power of the Lord outran King Ahab's chariot as black clouds erupted over them. God's promises may at times be invisible. When they do finally appear, they may seem as small as a human hand. Yet the certainty of God's promise is, at the end, sufficient for prophets thereby to surpass the chariots of violent men.

10

LIVING OUT OUR CALLINGS

All the nations may walk
in the name of their gods;
we will walk in the name of the LORD
our God for ever and ever.

MICAH 4:5

STOP FIGHTING

The four glorious verses of Micah's kingdom promise close with a declaration that reminds us—as if we needed reminding—that the kingdom is promised, not present. It's kind of like the pregame huddle, where the team captain leads the players in a chant, getting everybody focused on the victory to come, and then they take the field with an imperative to get out there and make it happen: *Go-fight-win!*

The critical difference between the pregame ritual and Micah is that the prophetic vision of future victory doesn't compel us into new heights of effort and achievement to make it turn out the way we want it to. Micah doesn't say to the Israelites, "Let's get out there and make this last days thing happen! Leave it all on the field for worship, discipleship and evangelism. We're going 110 percent on justice, industry and nonaggression. And I want to see some hard-hitting dignity, prosperity and security out there!" Instead, he reminds us that the vision will come to pass by the power of the Lord, and no one else. That's why all those other nations can walk in the name of their gods, but we will walk in the Lord's name forever, even when doing so seems foolish or fruitless—because we trust that God will be faithful to his promises.

The previous chapters have explored what it means to live in light of the kingdom of God, welcoming from a distance the promised land that comes but is not yet here. The kingdom vision offered by Micah is one of comprehensive peace—with God, among nations and in community—and has a very particular shape. In other words, peace with God isn't just a nice feeling, but the activity of worship, discipleship and evangelism, and likewise with the attributes we've explored for peace among the nations and in community.

Micah's final declaration—"we will walk in the name of the Lord"—prevents us from turning these attributes of peace into an agenda, however. Walking in the Lord's name means that we live in the power of God—under the banner of the divine name, as it were. This means that we cannot transform Micah's vision into a list of things that good Christians should accomplish, because the point of the kingdom isn't our accomplishment. Rather, they are a picture of what we can expect to see: not only in the perfect kingdom to come, but also imperfectly today, emanating from lives that seek a comprehensive faithfulness to Christ and his kingdom.

This can be the hardest thing to accept, especially in a group of well-intentioned people who love Jesus and also live in powerful, wealthy countries. After all, those of us who do are poised and ready to go, and we have a lot of resources to bring to bear. But God's "power is made perfect in weakness" (2 Corinthians 12:9), and we err if we stray from the cross—which is the ultimate symbol of weakness—or seek to adorn it with "words of human wisdom" (1 Corinthians 1:17) that empty the cross of its might.

Micah's continuing prophecy, after his kingdom vision of chapter 4:1-5, confirms that God works through inefficient and surprising vehicles. "'In that day,' declares the Lord, 'I will gather the lame; I will assemble the exiles and those I have brought to grief. I will make the lame a remnant, those driven away a strong nation'"—and he continues with promises of God's dominion and Jerusalem's glory restored (Micah 4:6-8). For us, this should serve as a stark reminder that the kingdom of God is not brought about by conquest and force (for example, John 18:36).

The prophet's recalibration concerns more than just our methods. It's about how we envision our fundamental orientation to a fallen world and the kingdom to come. As I described in chapter two, Western Christians, especially us younger activist types, tend to live lives patterned after hero stories, where the object of great worth is guarded by a terrible monster who must be defeated. But if this is our approach to the kingdom of God—as if it is a prize we obtain after overcoming the demon of sex trafficking or nuclear weapons or environmental degradation or whatever—then Satan has already won. For every blow we land on the jaw of this or that evil is actually a hammer stroke forging the shackles around our theological imagination, binding us to the idea that the kingdom is won through human power. It is not. Our job is not to win the victory, but to *expose* through our lives that the victory has been won on our behalf. And as a result, we will see shoots of God's kingdom erupt in our midst.

Paradoxically, this exposure requires even more work, commitment and spiritual strength than it does to tackle overt demons. And as we do not let the devil set the terms of our duel, we do not shy away from particular conflicts or renounce tactical measures. Jesus himself outlines some "exposure" tactics in the Sermon on the Mount: when you are struck, turn the other cheek; if you are robbed, give your robber the extra you have. Show your trust in God through actions that eschew normal strategies of self-preservation. The strength of such tactics derives from the fact that they require overcoming our truest enemy, which is ourselves, and that in us that hates God.

We see these tactics in action in the nonviolent resistance of people like Martin Luther King Jr. The goal of the civil rights movement was not to take the government by force, but to undeniably reveal the God-given humanity of African Americans. This could not have been achieved through force, because in the very act of becoming combatants, those in the movement would have allowed themselves to be dehumanized by their opponents. Instead, they put skin on the type of self-sacrifice, love and service that simply could not exist if there were no cross of Christ. A government armed with water cannons was impotent against the power of God that poured through the protesters like a mighty stream.

Such examples should challenge us as activist-minded Christians. Are we truly beginning with Christ, his call and his kingdom, rather than reacting to the manifold problems that plague our world? What does it mean, in practical terms, to expose the victory of God rather than to seek to win it on the Divine's behalf? How do we accept our roles as bit players and uncredited extras in a drama in which Jesus Christ is the only protagonist and hero?

A guide to these questions, I'd suggest, can be found not in any cutting-edge church trend, but in the shape of the life of an elder brother in Christ, recently gone to his reward.

THE RECTOR OF LANGHAM PLACE

To my wife and me, the Reverend Dr. John R. W. Stott will always be "Uncle John"—the avuncular honorific by which he was known to thousands of friends around the world. John Stott, who died in July

2011, was an Anglican clergyman and evangelical leader with a global reputation: in 2005, *TIME* magazine named him one of the world's one hundred most influential people, recognizing the impact that his lifetime of writing and speaking had had on several generations of Christians around the world. I had the privilege of serving as his study assistant from 2005 to 2006, alongside him and his indefatigable secretary of more than fifty years, Frances Whitehead.

Uncle John's passing has generated a great deal of reflection about his legacy. This is a question that I have often asked myself and one that tends to be asked of me whenever my time with him comes up in conversation: "What did you learn from him?" In truth, I am still learning lessons from my time at Uncle John's side, and I trust that I will continue to do so as I grow and mature in our Lord.

His significance for my generation of Christians, however, is that his apprehension of Christ's supremacy and singularity led him to model a comprehensive embrace of vocation, or calling.

First, Uncle John was a man obsessed with Jesus Christ. The focus of his ministry was Christ's gospel, centered on the redemptive work of the cross. It was his all in all. I took from him a new appreciation for Christ's glory and honor, especially in preaching. The pulpit at All Soul's Church, where he pastored for more than a quarter century, has a small plaque that only the preacher can see, reminding the pulpiteer that he or she has one job: "Sir, we would like to see Jesus" (John 12:21). Everything else for which he was known and which he cared about—pioneering ministry techniques; a concern for social justice decades ahead of his time, in evangelical circles; prolific writing; an anticolonial love for the Majority World; engagement with contemporary issues of public concern—was a direct and necessary consequence of his love for Jesus Christ.

Second, Uncle John's concern for Jesus, as the author and perfecter of his faith, manifested itself through his rich embrace of vocation. Throughout his life, he consistently sought to *be and do no more or less* than what he believed Christ had called him to. In other words, he sought to inhabit completely the space and time defined by God's call on his life. He accepted that space and time as the arena in which he faithfully worked out his salvation with fear and trembling, trusting that it was God who worked in him "to will and to act in order to fulfill his good purpose" (Philippians 2:13 NIV 2011).

For John Stott, the call to Christian discipleship entailed the call to be a pastor. He did not pursue this career because no other opportunities availed themselves. To the contrary, he had an exceptional intellect and a gift for communication, which opened many options for him to pursue what would have been career-advancing moves by any professional standard: diplomat, academic leader, bishop. But these opportunities for professional gain did not align with his sense of calling as a local pastor. Instead, he served All Souls Church, Langham Place, for three decades as curate and rector. When he finally stepped down to pursue a more global ministry, the second half of his life's work retained all the hallmarks of the pastorate—preaching, discipleship and evangelism—though his new parish was the global church.

Accepting this calling meant accepting its limitations. This trait is perhaps best symbolized by the fact that, despite a love for travel and an increasingly global consciousness, he spent virtually his entire life in the few square miles of Marylebone, the neighborhood in London's West End where his father had practiced medicine. During his tenure as curate and rector of All Souls, and afterward as rector emeritus, he lived at 12 Weymouth Street, spending six decades a short walk from his church and mere blocks from the house where he was raised.

Today, many younger Christians are rediscovering the importance of *place* to the Christian life, reacting in part against the geographic dislocation of a highly mobile society and the placelessness that much digital technology seems to offer, from mobile phones to cloud computing. Uncle John's example points to the truest significance of place: we are to be wherever it is Christ has called us to be—and contentedly so.

The limitations of Uncle John's calling were not only geographic but intimately personal as well. He remained celibate throughout his life, though not out of indifference to romantic love or to the joys of married life and family; later in life, he came to see his singleness as enabling the ministry to which God had called him.

Uncle John also lived an extraordinarily simple life, which equipped him to respond to life's quiet and small joys with profound appreciation. He lived frugally in a tiny apartment with a bedroom, an office and an utterly inadequate kitchenette, which left him delighted at any hospitality he received on his travels. He ate lightly and blandly, and thus rejoiced in a single square of chocolate for dessert and marveled at the taste of what was the rare luxury of a restaurant or home-cooked meal. He shopped rarely and grudgingly, maintaining the barest minimum of shirts, trousers and jackets necessary to do his work, and therefore received even small gifts, like a tie, with earnest gratitude.

It is easy to glorify the faithful departed, and if cringing is allowed in heaven, Uncle John is doing it to hear himself described so glowingly. He knew the sin in his own heart, and he protested that others would not praise him if they could only see it too. I do not imply that he was perfect. Rather, I base my praise on the outcome of his way of life (cf. Hebrews 13:7, the text both J. I. Packer and Tim Keller used for their eulogies to him). To whatever degree Uncle John strayed beyond the bounds of Christ's calling or failed to live into it fully, the whole of his life demonstrated a remarkably consistent record of faithfulness over time, which is sufficient for these purposes.

John Stott had one item on his lifetime to-do list: to know and proclaim the gospel of Jesus Christ. And in his single-minded dedication to this task, this single seed bore bushels of varied fruit. That is, as he occupied his calling as a disciple and a pastor to the utmost, his life yielded a diverse output that would be the envy of any score of activists. This is a profoundly countercultural example for a generation that tends to want to keep its options as open as possible and that is constantly offered a barrage of lifestyles.

There is an inherent challenge in Uncle John's example. He led an exceptional and extraordinary life marked by an extreme commitment to a very clear calling. This makes him exemplary, but what about us ordinary folks? Most of us haven't been given such God-given clarity about our vocations and aren't going to have anything like his impact. Our technological capacities, which place us in constant contact with every corner of the globe, pull us in a million directions at once. How would this work for the vast majority of us, whose vocation is a mosaic of commitments joining relational callings as spouses, children, parents, siblings with religious callings to service in our church families and with professional and civic callings in our jobs, neighborhoods and countries? Uncle John's is a difficult simplicity to emulate.

Also, he was a pastor, and it would be easy (though wrong) to infer from his example that some callings, particularly those in service of the official work of religion, are holier or worthier than others. What about those of us who work decidedly "secular" jobs as lawyers, laborers, plumbers, volunteers, stay-at-home parents, call-center receptionists, secretaries, retail clerks, accountants, middle management, janitors, salespersons, teachers and so on? Or those of us who, for one reason or another, fall outside the productivity cycle that society so esteems, whether because of joblessness, retirement, opportunity, age, physical ability or mental capacity? How are those of us whose lives are unlikely to be held up among the historic saints to make any meaningful use of his lesson in vocation?*

ACCEPTING LIMITATIONS

The breadth of Christian callings is as diverse as the number of believers who have been called, so no one-size-fits-all answer exists. With that caveat, however, the fundamental quality of divine calling is an acceptance of limitations. It is important to remember that your vocation is not what you do for a living, though that may be a significant or even dominant part of it. Your vocation is who you are called to be by God, and thus your vocation is to be like Jesus Christ through discipleship.

Here is a takeaway from John Stott that anyone can apply to her life, regardless of context or setting: he did not see the personal qualities of his discipleship—the fruit of the Holy Spirit—as distinct from his "professional" vocation as a pastor. Discipleship to Christ encompassed his life on every side, and *within* that space he lived out the particular calling of a pastor. The moral of the story is that we need to understand our discipleship to Christ as containing our whole life—no matter what job we do, relationships we maintain or abilities we do or don't have—rather than maintaining a "spiritual" part of life alongside everything else we care about.

The world is not ours; surely, that has been said often enough in these pages. But the corollary to the truth that we are not everywhere and everything is that we are somewhere and something. We inhabit the portion God gives us. Vocations have, and impart,

---

*To begin with, we can avail ourselves of a surge of interest in vocation, as evidenced by recent titles like Amy Sherman's *Kingdom Calling* (InterVarsity Press, 2011) and the work of groups like the Washington Institute for Faith, Vocation, and Culture. But vocation is the work of a lifetime, quite literally. So we should not be surprised if the answers require some sustained attention.

boundaries. To be called to *this* means not being called to *that*, and vice versa. An acceptance of calling therefore means a curtailing of some possibilities for our lives. For example, we do this with marriage when we forsake all others, as traditional vows have it.

It is similar as we follow Christ, though discipleship carries the finality of death—the forsaking of life itself. When we are young, many roads stretch before us for the choosing. As we age, we pick certain forks in the path of life. The number of future possibilities narrows until, at the moment of death, all choices are replaced with the singularity of mortality. To embrace vocation is to embrace mortality's singularity out of time, so to speak, though it is not our own death that we choose, but Christ's. Because being his disciple means sharing in his death through baptism, living out our Christian vocation means cutting off all possibilities for our lives other than those to which he calls us, "for you died, and your life is now hidden with Christ in God" (Colossians 3:3).

I wonder what it would look like if we could channel this generation's activist impulses through the limiting discipline of vocation? It might inoculate us from the fleeting faddishness of causes and the threat of faith-based burnout, because we would begin to live out our sorrow over a suffering world through the lifelong work of discipleship. It would also enrich and deepen our activism, taking actions that are often conducted at the periphery of our lives—liking a group on Facebook, re-tweeting some pithy quote, foregoing a coffee, sporting socially conscious shoes—and drawing the concern motivating them into the core of lives that are hidden in Christ.

WHAT HAVE YOU BEEN GIVEN?

I know firsthand how difficult this task is. I find myself pulled in dozens of different directions on any given week, tempted to spread myself on many different ventures and projects. I see a world in need of salvation and desperately want to give it. But salvation has not been given to me to impart.

What, then, has been given to me? Nothing I can contribute has come to me through my own effort. Though I have worked hard, it is God who has given me the strength to do so. The question of how I will respond to the chorus of crying needs of the world—before which I am like a man standing at the edge of the Pacific Ocean, holding a small sponge—is not based on what the world needs but on how God has equipped me to give.

So, if I stop to think about it, here is what God has given me:

- The Lord Jesus Christ, in his incarnation, cross, resurrection and church, and the eternal peace won through him, in which I have a share through the grace of receiving repentant awareness of my sin, and baptism in faith;
- ordination to preach and teach the gospel, by the laying on of hands;
- a loving wife who is my partner and colaborer in Christ;
- the stability and joys of family formed by faith, blood and marriage;
- good physical and mental health (enabled, in part, by living in a place with health care and clean water, air and earth);
- certain capacities for thought, analysis, communication and humor;
- a heart that naturally breaks to see others afraid or in pain;
- the rights and responsibilities of my American citizenship;
- the security and freedom derived from living in a society governed, however imperfectly, by the rule of law;
- the capabilities and opportunities afforded by my education;
- the love of friends and the support of colleagues in diverse fields around the world;

- financial resources built through work and savings and a stable source of income (which cannot be extricated from complicity in unjust economic structures);

- breath in my lungs today.

If done honestly, such cataloging is cringe inducing. It can seem vainglorious to list our qualities. But I recall Uncle John's frequent comment that humility "is another word for honesty . . . not pretending to be other than we are, but acknowledging the truth about what we are."[1] There is nothing virtuous in pretending we have what we do not or that we do not have what we actually do. I am conscious in writing this list that I have earned none of these things, and yet I enjoy their benefits.

So, what does my list tell me about who I am? I can see a natural priority of vocational commitments to discipleship, gospel proclamation, my marriage, a community of relationships and a concern for peace and security.

I am also conscious that I enjoy material and physical blessings that put me far above the global average—and stratospherically beyond the world's most destitute. I benefit—on a daily basis, as well as from the accretion of privilege in history—from the injustice of social structures that impart status and power based on arbitrary and contingent realities, like my whiteness and maleness. I cannot claim that benefiting from injustice is a gift of God. How can I give account for the entirety of my life?

Perhaps the way forward is to understand ourselves as *stewards* of all that we have received. What does your list look like? Some may enjoy gifts of fantastic power, wealth and status. Others will have more modest lists. For those whose lives are filled with sorrow, the list of God's gifts may seem short and meager. Regardless of our respective lists' specific and various content, their purpose is to be poured out for Christ's kingdom and glory through service in a broken and sinful world. We hold our gifts in our souls and minds and bodies and hands and relationships.

If we were not followers of Jesus Christ, we might imagine them to be our possessions, over which we stand sovereign, free to dispose of as we wish. But Christ's call compels us. He stands before us and behind us, to either side of us, above us and below us. So we must say of our own lives, as many churches sing during the monetary offering, that "all things come of thee, O Lord, and of thine own have we given thee."

Each of us will have different gifts from God, but every vocation can be offered for Christ's kingdom. Micah's vision provides the picture of what this looks like.

Peace with God. We have been given a relationship with God: are we devoting ourselves to the concrete behavior of regular *worship,* active *discipleship* and *evangelism*? Do we share with others the joy of the gospel? Are we doing what we can to encourage the same in our relationships of care—family, friends, colleagues? Are we waking every morning with the recognition that the day is a gift of God and that until we die or until he brings us to rest in the night, every second and every breath should be an offering to the Lord?

Peace among the nations. Many of us have been given citizenship and a voice in the workings of our respective nations. Are we employing any rights and privileges, as opportunity permits, in the service of *justice, industry* and *nonaggression*? Do we give our support in finances and time to efforts that work for peace among the nations, according to the measure we have received? Do we consistently seek to pour out any national status accorded to us, using our status to undermine the imbalanced and unjust structures that create status in the first place? Where we are disadvantaged, do we refuse to be defined as victims?

Peace in community. Each of us has been given a particular community in which we live, both geographically proximate and, for many, technologically global. Do we comprehensively stand for human *dignity, prosperity* and *security* in these communities? Do we renounce or redirect gain that we receive from injustice, employing any benefit we might receive in the service of those who are oppressed? Where we do not occupy a privileged status, do we conduct ourselves in a way that forces oppressors to encounter our full humanity, our being made in the image of God? Do we stand firm in the face of unjust threat? Do we refuse that anyone in our community be made to fear?

Fundamentally, do we trust that God's will will be done and God's kingdom come on earth as it is in heaven? And with all that we are, do we welcome that kingdom from a distance, across the opaque span of a creation that groans for redemption? To the degree that we are able to do these things, I hope and trust that the particular giftedness of this generation will be deeply rooted in the gospel and enjoy a long harvest.

RECONSIDERING CHRISTIAN PUBLIC ENGAGEMENT

I began my ongoing pilgrimage toward the kingdom of God as an activist, and though I have taken on other vocations along the way, I have remained an activist throughout. While I believe that a fundamental task for this generation is to develop a vocation-based activist sensibility, integrating such impulses deeply into the Christian life as described above, I also know that explicit ventures in faith-based activism—projects, organizations, campaigns and the like—are not going away. Nor should they. That is, Christians and the church should be engaged in deliberate activity for the public common good—in all its manifestations.

A word is necessary here regarding the lively current debate over the mission of the church in the public square. I do not fit squarely within any of the competing camps, which both require and deserve a better summary than I can offer here. I fall somewhere between those who would transform the world and those who reject the church's engagement in public affairs (with apologies for the imprecision of this description). The world is not ours to change, transform or save. We do not know the date we will die, and this alone should humble the grandeur of our plans. Moreover, whatever we are able to accomplish in our time, another may tear down or use for evil in another day. The change we exert within a society is never permanent, and we must discount any Enlightenment sensibility of inevitable progress, because the final judgment of God stands as an impassable rupture in the continuity between the specific goods of these latter days and the good of the kingdom. The good that the church and Christians can accomplish in the present should be viewed as a temporary phenomenon of faithfulness, like sweat resulting from vigorous exercise. (This doesn't mean that we shouldn't build to last as much as we're able, though, nor that we should shirk from reforming institutions.)

At the same time, good done outside the bounds of the church—by Christians or not—is still real good, double entendre intended. I am baffled by those who willfully deny the historical fact that followers of Christ and Christianity itself—and even the much-maligned Christendom—have made life better for Christians and non-Christians alike. Christian love built hospitals and schools, freed slaves, emancipated women and protected children, and laid the philosophical groundwork for modern human rights as we know them. (Of course, Christianity has also done the evil polar opposite of all these goods, which we have to account for too.)

These accomplishments are not invalidated by virtue of their imperfection. The fall corrupted all politics, but not all politics is equally corrupt. It is the height of arrogance to assert blithely that all human society outside the church is morally depraved. (Go pastor in North Korea for a while and then try to make the same claim.) This is especially contemptible if such assertions come from individuals whose ability to speak freely and publish such declarations results directly from living in a culture with Christian roots.

Perhaps it is helpful to distinguish between what the church *must* do in all situations with the good that the church *may* do in others. That is, the church in all times and all places must worship God, preach the Scriptures, live lives befitting followers of Jesus Christ and anticipate the coming kingdom with works of righteousness and justice. But if the church finds itself in a context where its faithful obedience may yield public fruit that shapes the common good, on what basis should it decide not to share that broader blessing of God? Where the church has influence—such as the United States—it cannot turn away from its responsibility. So, if it is dark in America, where are the bearers of the Light? *Stewardship* is thus the operative term guiding Christian public engagement, as with vocational activism.

TWO FAMILIAR TACTICS

Unfortunately, we do not always excel at activism intended to illuminate our public square. Too often we assume that doing good in public simply means using one of two well-worn tactics.

The first is *mobilization*, or some variation of Vietnam-era protest work: unite a bunch of people behind a common cause to fix a social problem. The presupposition behind the mobilization tactic is that the powers (and problems) that be will respond to the concerted desire of the people. In church circles, this manifests as attempts to engage the large numbers of people who self-identify as Christian. The church is, among other things, a group of people who purport to believe similar things about right and wrong. It therefore appears to be a natural site for activist organizers who fantasize about the impact that those numbers could have if directed to the same petition/protest march/letter-writing campaign/elected-official visit/fundraising drive/etc.

Donors—especially from the secular, cause-focused world—can regard religious communities as rentable constituencies, which doesn't help the situation. Those who are personally unfamiliar with the life of a faith community, Christian or otherwise, often imagine Sunday services to be a place where the robotic dogmatic voluntarily gather each week to receive their political marching orders in mysterious theological code. Why not, therefore, simply plug in a sermon extolling this or that cause?

The other standard model for religious activism is that of the *moral arbiter*. This model also hearkens to a bygone past, but it's Christendom, rather than Vietnam. The moral arbiter position presupposes that the Christian church has a unique and authoritative moral voice in the public square—that is, that when a group of clergy or denominational officials say something about a controversial issue, it's meaningful. The mainline Protestant denominations have been notorious for employing this tactic, issuing declarations and moral imperatives on every conceivable topic and expecting elected officials to act accordingly. These declarations are often freighted with the adjective *prophetic*, which increasingly seems to mean an order given by someone without power to someone with it.

An evangelical variant of the moral arbiter tactic has sprung up like kudzu over the past decade. It involves taking a cause not usually associated with political conservatives, which a majority of evangelicals continue to be, branding it with the evangelical label, maybe through a signed letter from evangelical leaders, and then attempting to use the "man bites dog" shock value for the purposes of political positioning.

The terrific irony of this tactic is that it pays for its campaigns out of a stolen checking account, because its efficacy depends wholly on the political capital built up by the Religious Right—that is, the belief that evangelicals are a political force to be reckoned with—even though it is most often employed for purposes that would make Jerry Falwell want to tear his hair out. (Full transparency: the Two Futures Project has profited from this very trend.) After about ten years of this, most media and elected officials have wised up, and our broad new agenda doesn't surprise anyone anymore. As a result, evangelical political salience has dropped, which in my estimation is a good thing, since it requires us to engage public issues from a deeply and clearly biblical basis, rather than relying simply on the political cachet of the evangelical label and a few representative endorsements.

You may guess from my tone that I am less than enthusiastic about either approach, so I should note for the sake of balance that both the mobilization and the moral arbiter models can be used effectively. Whether you like the Religious Right or not, you have to respect their strategic vision. They worked for decades on the ground, in politically strategic locations, building a grass-roots constituency that cared (and still cares) about hot-button social issues like abortion, same-sex marriage and prayer in schools. On the moral arbiter side, declarations like the US Conference of Catholic Bishops' 1983 pastoral letter on nuclear weapons are known to have had a significant impact on relevant policymakers and military officers. More recently, the "Circle of Protection" has stood with the poor in the face of potentially devastating government budget cuts.

However, despite a short list of tactical successes, it is lamentable that the Christian activist imagination is often a quiver with only two arrows in it. It makes for bad activism. Worse, it makes for terrible Christianity, because these tactics begin with the shape of the political problem and then attempt to employ the faith as a tool in response.

A NEW VISION FOR CHRISTIAN ACTIVISM

In that spirit, I suggest a complete recalibration for Christian methods of activism, oriented toward the kingdom of God and rooted in vocation.

The traditional activist approach asks, *How can public goods be obtained using Christianity?* Our recalibrated approach, which I will call "kingdom-oriented activism," asks instead, *What unique and authentic contribution can the Christian church make to the public square?* The distinction hinges on whether we begin with the problem at hand or with the nature of the kingdom that is coming and which is already here. If the church is going to engage issues of public concern and the common good, it must do so in a way that does not compromise the fundamental nature of its power, which derives completely from the cross of Christ and the Holy Spirit. Therefore, its methods of public engagement should hold to the character of its divine calling, lest the church be turned into a mere meaty political apparatus (a transformation that has been common in Christian history).

Toward that end, the following typology proposes nine possible modes of distinctively Christian activism, or methods of engagement regarding public goods.

Priestly, or intervening through corporate and individual prayer and fasting for the public good. Prayer and fasting are often skipped over, unnoticed, in the development of activist campaigns, which want to focus on actions that "really get things done." Yet such actions, more than anything else the church can do, declare our confidence in the power of God. Prayer also receives explicit scriptural endorsement in Paul's urging to offer "requests, prayers, intercession and thanksgiving . . . for kings and all those in authority, that we may live peaceful and quiet lives in all godliness and holiness" (1 Timothy 2:1-2). This is not simply prayer to baptize our activity, but rather genuine searching for God's will and requesting his intervention and strength.

Didactic, or the church's teaching role toward its membership. In all but the most extreme circumstances, governmental policies should not be preached from the pulpit. This is not because the church is indifferent to politics. Rather, it is to reserve space for the proclamation of the Word of God, the retelling of the gospel and corporate worship and fellowship. We have six days to labor in the trenches, and God is God then too; it is not too much to ask to preserve an hour weekly for teaching the story of Jesus Christ. Biblical teaching is also activist activity, albeit indirectly, because it creates citizens of the kingdom who will exercise more faithfulness in their earthly citizenship. The same applies for the teachers of teachers: I like the way Russell Moore, dean of theology at Southern Baptist Seminary, describes his job as training pastors to shape the theological imagination of their congregations, so that the people of God build instincts of natural delight at what God delights in.

Architectural, or the building of institutions and ventures that contribute to the public good. This can be the direct work of the church, as when a congregation houses a food bank or soup kitchen. Whenever possible, however, I suggest that such efforts are best served by pushing them out of the congregation and into entities specially dedicated to the task, as when congregations spin off nonprofit ventures. The practices of church governance are not always suited to running business enterprises, whether for-profit or nonprofit. Additionally, by pushing such efforts outside the congregation's walls, the church creates more space for Christians to exercise marketplace-oriented vocations. This model would also apply to any business that does "business as it ought to be," as DEMDACO founder Dave Kiersznowski puts it. A business that consciously anticipates the kingdom of God in its practices is one of the most powerful forms of Christian public engagement.

Judicial, or participation in public discussion and debate, as a stakeholder whose bottom line is the moral good and human flourishing to the glory of God, rather than any particular partisan, military or economic interest. This would be a welcome respite from Christian cheerleading for one faction or another. In concrete terms, this means scholarship, publication, debate and advocacy as Christians in a pluralist public square, arguing the value of Christian positions for a society that does not take for granted Christian truth claims.

Prophetic, or the sort of action and speech that seeks to reveal truth, indifferent to political calculus or efficacy. The ancient Israelite prophets theatrically embodied the judgment of God against their day and time—for example, Jeremiah buying land as invaders were poised to take over Jerusalem or Isaiah walking around naked and shoeless for three years as a sign against invading forces. (Maybe the "nudes, not nukes" protesters were on to something after all.) The Old Testament standard for a prophet was one who spoke God's own words, regardless of the cost, and who demonstrated a limitless commitment to that truth. After Christ, we no longer have the equivalent of biblical prophets. But a similar spirit is demonstrated by, for example, protestors who break into nuclear bases and hit bombers with sledgehammers until they are arrested. Such means tend not to be especially helpful by the standards of more strategic, moderate approaches toward the same goals; they can even harm "the cause" by casting every advocate as a radical. But such activists are brave and single-hearted, and they reveal something of the truth of God.

Pastoral, or caring for the lives and souls of people who exercise authority in public matters, like elected officials and their staffs, policymakers, bureaucrats, military leaders and so on. Such individuals are often asked to disengage their consciences and morality to be better apparatuses of the systems that they serve. It can be easy to forget that there is a Lord above Caesar, and people who live in the public eye desperately need individual relationships of trust and care with Christians—whether or not they are professional pastors. We should note that such relationship building is not a pretext for lobbying, but rather an equipping of the saints who are called to exercise fidelity in their vocational context.

Diplomatic, or the direct ambassadorial work of gospel peacemaking. Christians are called to be bearers of God's ministry of reconciliation, which we believe can break down any wall. So there is no terrain too hostile for Christians to enter openly with the hope that the relationship will open onto the reconciliatory offer of the gospel. Putting such a face on our faith is especially important when millions worldwide perceive no daylight between Christianity and American foreign policy.

Militant, or employing the infrastructure and numbers of people in churches toward deliberate political ends. This is classic mobilization, whether in boycott, protest, voting or other methods. Because it employs coercive tactics, this is the most perilous option for the soul of a church that exists not by might but by the spirit of God. As such, it should be employed only in the face of undeniable injustice. Examples might include Christian efforts toward the abolition of slavery and the use of churches in the Underground Railroad, the church's participation in the American civil rights movement and some South African churches' leadership in the fight against apartheid as well as global churches' participation in the boycott of and divestment from that system.

Sectarian, or withdrawal. When confronted with evil so radical that it is beyond reform, there may be occasions when the church's most faithful testimony and powerful action is to withdraw and refuse participation, because even to engage the opponent is to bestow legitimacy on it. This is a measure of last resort. The Barmen Declaration comes to mind, in which the German Confessing Church simply refused to participate in National Socialism, because the demands of Nazism directly contradicted the imperatives of Christian teaching and discipleship.

I do not intend for this typology of kingdom-oriented tactics for Christian activism to be a list of mutually exclusive options. That is, the Christian nonprofit leader who runs a successful *architectural* venture may also have *pastoral* relationships with policy-makers through a private Bible study and write articles that make a *judicial* contribution to the public debate over a particular issue. A Christian employee at an insurance company can approach his work with a *diplomatic* spirit, pray regularly in *priestly* intercession for his elected officials and benefit from his pastor's *didactic* teaching of the Word of God.

I have a threefold purpose in proposing this type of list. First, I hope that it might help to expand our imaginations about what constitutes activism, allowing deeper integration of such actions into our lives. We can do so much better—and be so much more faithful to the gifts we have received—than our reflexive defaulting to mobilization or moral declarations.

Second, I hope that this list might help existing activist efforts think more theologically about their activities. What sort of activism are they engaged in already? Where might they expand? What tactical models are most faithful and effective to their particular callings? For example, a Christian group desiring to change policy in Washington might realize that it has regarded certain individuals or groups as enemies, rather than as human beings, and thus seek to understand them better by developing friendships carrying a *pastoral* concern. An action-oriented group might become aware that it has completely neglected prayer and *priestly* intercession. Those seeking to engage churches might recognize that their teaching materials seek to exploit the *didactic* mission of the church, rather than benefiting it, and thus need to be revised.

Third, and most important, I hope that a model of activism based in the distinctive practices of the church and individual Christians will remind us that we labor in light of a kingdom that we have not established and that we cannot build with permanence. At best we can steward the time and space that God has allotted us. By grounding our compassion and action within Christ's invincible church, against which the armies of hell will someday fall, we ensure that we are working in the right direction and for the right reasons.

NOT FIGHTING THE BATTLE OF NEW ORLEANS

In July 2011, Natalie and I moved from Nashville to Toronto, where she took her first university teaching position after finishing her doctorate in theology. The move was a hard one because we had set down good roots in Tennessee: we left behind a church family we loved dearly, a wonderful circle of friends and a vibrant city whose treasures we had come to know well.

The move was also timely, however, not least in its natural development of Natalie's clear vocation as a teacher. For me, the shift across the border has opened up increased possibilities for the international focus of the Global Task Force on Nuclear Weapons of the World Evangelical Alliance, which I chair. Additionally, after more than four years of eating, drinking and breathing only nuclear weapons, our dislocation has afforded the opportunity for some self-reflection and consideration of broader questions.

One interesting aspect of moving to Canada has been observing Canadian public debate, which differs considerably from that in America. For example, Canadians have engaged in a surprisingly vigorous argument about how to approach the bicentennial of the War of 1812. This would be a nonissue if Canadian troops, then a part of Great Britain, had not burned down the American White House as part of the war.

How should this historical event be commemorated? The Canadians are proud of being Canadians, so they want to remember their heritage. But they are also kind and generous, and they don't especially want to wave a bygone act of presidential arson in the face of their closest neighbor and ally. What to do? (One wishes that all international conundrums were so benign.)

The War of 1812 brings to mind another incident, at the war's close. On January 8, 1815, British and American troops clashed in the Battle of New Orleans. The irony—sad, really—of one of America's greatest historical military victories is that it didn't need to happen. The Treaty of Ghent, which ended the war, had been signed several weeks prior, on Christmas Eve 1814. Today, the news would be all over Twitter, but back then, slow communications meant that the troops didn't find out the war was over until February, long after the smoke had cleared from New Orleans.

There's a lesson in this for Christians, and I'm not the first preacher to draw it: we often fight unnecessary battles. But unlike the troops at New Orleans, we are without excuse. We have received the news of victory, of the end of conflict, of peace. We are free. The proclamation shouts from every cross and crucifix. It whispers in every act of Christian sacrifice and love.

There is no need to leave further casualties on the field of a superfluous war. We do not have to imagine that the battle hinges on our effort. Instead, we are free, like the Israelite militia in Micah's day—not to rest on our laurels, but to return to our homes and fields, and there to hammer swords into shapes more suited to breaking ground than bodies. The battle is won, the conflict done, the anthem sung. And the kingdom comes.

STUDY GUIDE

The World Is Not Ours to Save is intended for group study in a variety of formats. Depending on your available time, you might consider the following suggested structures: single session (entire book), two sessions (part 1 and part 2), five sessions (chapter 1, chapters 2-3, chapters 4-5, chapters 6-8, chapters 9-10) or ten sessions (one per chapter).

PART ONE: THE LIMITS OF ACTIVISM

Chapter 1: The World Is Not Ours to Save

1. Tyler begins the book by listing Christian involvement in a "myriad of world-improving causes." Where do you see Christians doing good in today's culture?

2. Can you identify examples of "a faith that is focused outward, engaged with culture, concerned with authenticity and activist in its orientation"? What does the book see as the strengths and weaknesses of this type of faith? Do you agree with this diagnosis?

3. Tyler focuses in particular on a rising generation of Christians. How are today's Christians different than—or similar to—those of previous generations?

4. Have you experienced or seen instances of "cause fatigue" among Christians?

5. In describing his conversion, Tyler writes that "often it is the questions you are asked, not the answers you are given, that prove most important in the long term." What's the most important question you've ever been asked?

Chapter 2: Don't Be a Hero

1. What does this chapter identify as the three aspects of hero-focus that will undermine our doing good?

2. Tyler writes that "our heroic impulse also reveals something dark and sinister about human nature." What is the shadow side of heroism? Do you agree with this argument, and why?

3. "The Angriest Activist" section questions the prevalent Christian focus on "making a difference" in the world. "*Impact* is value neutral. It's a concept based on degree of influence rather than quality." Where do you want to make a difference? Does this desire ever conflict with holistic Christlikeness in your life? How are you able to bring work and discipleship into balance?

4. Did this chapter change how you read the story of David and Goliath? How might the insight that "everybody's a David" affect your reading of other Scripture passages?

5. "In a way, the story of Christ is the only story we know how to tell . . . we just tell it in thousands upon thousands of ways." Where have you seen Christ-figures in books, television, movies, theater, etc.? How do they illuminate your understanding of Jesus?

Chapter 3: Broken Beyond Our Repair

1. "The promise of our progressive, modern age is that the world is subject to repair, given the right willpower and tools." Do Christians believe in this promise? Does the culture at large? Why might someone believe or disbelieve in the promise of progress? What does Tyler describe as the failures of this assessment?

2. In the section on the Hiroshima bridge, Tyler describes a personal experience of the world's irreparable brokenness. Where have you seen this brokenness?

3. What does *oikonomia* mean, and how is it applicable to today's global crises?

4. What does Tyler identify as the limits of individual activism?

5. What is "sinner's prayer activism"? Do you think Tyler's assessment is fair, or not? Have you seen videos like the one described here? How do you tend to react to this kind of appeal?

6. Tyler concludes by talking about "incarnating a love that lunges to stretch across a brokenness that it cannot repair." What would this look like in your own life? How would a recognition of this brokenness change the way you live? Did the closing section of the chapter leave you encouraged, hopeless, or something in between?

Chapter 4: Fear God

1. Think of some popular Christian causes. What is the implicit (or explicit) witness to God made by their work? What's the connection between the change they seek and the God they serve?

2. Tyler suggests that when we are confronted with difficult Bible passages (like Deuteronomy 2:32-36), we pick one of four options: (1) hate God, (2) become monsters, (3) deny that God is really like this or (4) fear God. Do you agree? Have you experienced any of these reactions in your readings of Scripture? How else might you encounter such texts?

3. "The goodness of God is so alien in its holiness that human life must encounter it in awestruck fear and perhaps something resembling terror and horror. We are left with a God who in no way may be domesticated to serve any earthly project." How do you respond to this portrayal of God? How does it affect Christian causes?

4. What is the theological rationale for illustrating the atomic bombings of Hiroshima and Nagasaki, which killed hundreds of

thousands of people, by focusing on a handful of individuals? How did you react to the story of the Nakazawas and the Taodas?

5. How does Tyler claim that a greater understanding of God has transformed his anti-nuclear activism? How does the reality of God challenge and/or support your own personal commitments? Where do you see the balance of "efficacy" and "fidelity" at work in your life?

Chapter 5: Take These Snakes

1. What does this chapter identify as the "world's most intractable problem"? Do you agree with this assessment?

2. What do you think about the Israeli-Palestinian conflict? Regardless of your personal beliefs, describe as fairly as possible each side's own justification for its cause. Does it matter for us to understand "the other side," no matter how much we disagree with it?

3. How does Tyler suggest that we should read John 3:16: "for God so loved the world"? Interpreting this passage in light of the story of the bronze serpent from Numbers 21, what does he say it would mean for God to "take away the snakes" of the problems that plague us? How does God show love, instead?

4. How did you react to the story of Daoud Nassar and the Tent of Nations farm? What is the theological justification for "refusing to be enemies"? Why is it powerful? Where could you refuse enmity in your own context?

5. Tyler writes that "in certain places . . . the kingdom comes close enough that even the most myopic of the faithful can begin to discern its outlines." Have you ever seen the outlines of the kingdom of God? How did you recognize it?

6. In *The Gulag Archipelago*, the late Russian author, dissident and Nobel laureate Aleksandr Solzhenitsyn wrote: "If only there were evil people somewhere insidiously committing evil deeds, and it were necessary only to separate them from the rest of us and destroy them. But the line dividing good and evil cuts through the heart of every human being. And who is willing to destroy a piece of his own heart?" What in your own heart contributes to the problems you want to solve?

PART TWO: A DEEPER CALLING

Chapter 6: The Peaceable Kingdom

1. What's the difference between trying to save the world and living in light of the world-saving work of Christ?

2. Tyler writes that "the contours of the coming kingdom call to us from the future, like the memory of a reality that doesn't yet exist. When we respond to this call, the present is shaped as an echo or shadow or trace of what will be." This is "welcoming the kingdom at a distance." How does your understanding of God's coming kingdom shape the way you live now?

3. Read Micah 4:1-5 out loud. What jumps out at you in the passage?

4. What do you think when you hear the word *peace*? Do you think your views are similar to the majority or the minority of other Christians? Of your fellow citizens? Have you ever encountered a Christian "allergy to peace"? What did it look like, and how did you respond?

5. What does Tyler mean by "True War"? How would you begin to live this out?

Chapter 7: Peace with God

1. Why does Tyler use Coventry Cathedral to frame a chapter about peace with God? How could you apply any of the lessons from Coventry in your own context?

2. According to the chapter, what is the heart of "worship[ing] in truth"? Why is worship so important to Christian activists? How does worship change our perception of the world?

3. Tyler identifies reconciliation, unity and vocation as three key areas of discipleship. Briefly describe the significance of each area. How are these practices taught in your church? Where do you need the most growth, both individually and as a community?

4. Tyler describes Coventry Cathedral as a rare exception to the tendency to prioritize evangelism over peace, or vice versa. Do you agree with this assessment? How are evangelism and peace related? Can you describe a community that manages to maintain a passionate commitment to both?

5. Cast a vision for what your church or community might look like with a renewed focus on worship, discipleship and evangelism as three biblical markers of peace with God. What steps can you take personally to begin living this out?

Chapter 8: Peace Among the Nations

1. Were you already aware of the threat posed by nuclear weapons? Why does Tyler use the possibility of nuclear terrorism to open this chapter?

2. According to the chapter, what is the relationship between justice and peace among the nations? What is a biblical definition of justice? Based on this definition, identify examples of both justice and injustice in public life, from your own com-

munity to international relations. Does justice require that the powerful be humbled?

3. Why does Tyler interpret the biblical text of "beating swords into plowshares" through the lens of *industry*? How is industry important to peace?

4. Tyler tells the story of Dave and Demi Kiersznowski's company, DEMDACO, as an example of a "plowshares business." Using concrete examples, what makes DEMDACO different from other companies? How could this example help transform your own workplace—whether you are the CEO or an intern?

5. Are your views on foreign affairs informed by a theological commitment to nonaggression? What would it mean for you to live out this commitment to peace? What does Tyler argue are the three implications of taking the "just war" tradition seriously?

Chapter 9: Peace in Community

1. Contrary to Micah's "linear vision" of peace with God and peace among the nations, the attributes of peace in community "occur simultaneously" in Micah 4:4. "Dignity, prosperity and security dance together, a perichoresis of earthly peace. Where dignity is, there too is prosperity and security. Remove either of the latter, and all collapse." Identify an issue in your city or town that involves dignity, prosperity and security.

2. The section on dignity emphasizes a balance between individual and community welfare. Where have you seen this balance succeed (or fail) in your local community?

3. What is the difference between prosperity as an aspect of peace in community and either "the prosperity gospel" or luxury? Do you see this positive, biblical prosperity in your context? How can Christians be committed to prosperity while maintaining

the lifestyle of simplicity and self-emptying generosity that the New Testament mandates?

4. What is the basis for the biblical injunction to "fear not"? What do you fear? Where do you see others living in fear?

5. "A man and his child, whom he loves, come to the Mountain River. There he stoops to bind himself with a chain of gold, that his child might walk free. Stop. Listen. We have heard this story elsewhere—other fathers, other children, other bindings, other emancipations." What stories do you think that Tyler is referring to here?

Chapter 10: Living Out Our Callings

1. "Are we truly beginning with Christ, his call and his kingdom, rather than reacting to the manifold problems that plague our world? What does it mean, in practical terms, to expose the victory of God rather than to seek to win it on the Divine's behalf?" Discuss these questions in your context.

2. What is vocation/calling? Did this chapter affect how you understand your own vocation?

3. Tyler writes that John Stott's zeal for Christ "led him to model a comprehensive embrace of vocation" by accepting limitations. Referring to John Stott's story, identify these limitations. What limitations might you need to embrace in your own sense of calling?

4. In the section "What Have You Been Given?" Tyler catalogs a list of personal gifts. Using this as an example, write your own list of gifts. Then go through the three categories of peace at the end of this section, asking and answering as a group how you can offer your gifts for God's kingdom.

5. What does Tyler identify as the "two familiar tactics" of Christian activism? Name examples of these tactics from your own experience. Do you think that non-Christians have a generally positive or negative view of Christian public engagement?

6. How would the proposed alternate typology of public faith (*priestly, didactic, architectural,* etc.) change your approach to living out your Christianity? Which types seem most suited to your gifts?

ACKNOWLEDGMENTS

I am deeply grateful to the family, friends and colleagues whose support has made this book possible.

Thanks to my agent, Erik Wolgemuth, and to my editor, Al Hsu, along with the team at InterVarsity Press, who believed in this project and who have been a joy to work with.

This book is orders of magnitude better due to those who read early manuscripts and gave comments: Matthew Lee Anderson, Brian Auten, Peter Greer, Scott Kauffman, Sean Palmer and Arielle Swarr. Thank you for the gift of your friendship. Whatever faults remain are greatly reduced by the gift of your time and wisdom.

A substantial portion of the book's reflections emerge out of my involvement in the anti-nuclear community, in which I have been privileged to enjoy extraordinary colleagues over the years, especially: Jonathan Granoff and David Cortright, for mentoring me; Barbara Green and T. C. Morrow from Faithful Security; and Amanda Kreps-Long, David Jones and particularly Adam Woods, who made the Two Futures Project possible.

My friend and inestimable colleague Jessica Wilbanks gets a triple heaping of gratitude for her expert feedback on the manuscript, her collegiality at Faithful Security and her invaluable contribution to 2FP.

The Fourth Freedom Forum provided a home for 2FP's work, and I am grateful for the leadership of Alistair Millar and Linda Gerber-Stellingwerf. We also enjoyed generous support from the Nuclear Threat Initiative (thanks to Carmen MacDougall, Cathy Gwin, Joan Rohlfing and Deborah Rosenblum), the Ploughshares Fund (thanks to Joe Cirincione and Naila Bolus) and the Skoll Global Threats Fund (thanks to Bruce Lowry, Kate Wilkinson and Larry Brilliant), among others, with particular gratitude to Alex Toma and Dini Merz.

Thanks to the staff, past and present, at the National Association of Evangelicals—Richard Cizik, Galen Carey, Leith Anderson, Heather Gonzales and Sarah Kropp, among others—who have been invaluable partners. I have also treasured my involvement with the global family of Christians through the Langham Partnership International, World Evangelical Alliance, Lausanne Movement and Council for Christian Approaches to Defense and Disarmament, especially Chris Wright, Geoff Tunnicliffe, Rosalee Velloso Ewell, Deb Fikes and Pierce Corden.

I cannot express enough gratitude to the pastors and leaders who invited me to share the Two Futures Project message with their congregations and communities. You know who you are, and I thank you. First Baptist Church, Palo Alto; Status Church, Orlando; the Plowshares Group at Wheaton College; and the Catalyst family also deserve special thanks for allowing me to work out the ideas that eventually formed the core of this book. This book records two relatively recent experiences that I had the privilege of joining in through the graciousness of Steve Haas, Todd Deatherege and Greg Khalil, as well as Peter Kuznick.

I am also grateful for those who blazed the trail that 2FP has trod: former secretary of state George Shultz, Senator Sam Nunn, former secretary of defense William Perry, Dr. Sid Drell and Ambassador Jim Goodby—as well as Jim Wallis, Ron Sider, Joel Hunter, David Gushee and Glen Stassen. I thank each of them for the example of their enduring moral courage and the gift of their friendship.

I did not know when I reengaged the work for nuclear security that my doing so would introduce me to Christians in the United States and around the world whom I now count among my greatest friends. Gabe Lyons and Cameron Strang were the earliest adopters of 2FP's message among a rising generation of leaders. Both showed astonishing generosity in using their resources and platforms to advance our cause: 2FP got its name around a conference table in the offices of Cameron's *Relevant* magazine and had its public debut at

Gabe's Q gathering. Both have become treasured friends. Without them, the Two Futures Project simply would not be.

The support of friends and colleagues in this community has sustained and inspired me, whether they knew it or not, including Leroy Barber, Mimi Barnard, Josh Benoit, Jeremy Blume, Shane Claiborne, Paul Corts, Andy Crouch, Margaret Feinberg and Leif Oines, Mark and Jan Foreman, Mark Galli, Steve Graves, Peter Greer, Sara and Troy Groves, C. J. Guinness, Jay Harren, Will Hinton, Chris and Phileena Heuertz, Bethany Hoang, Lynne Hybels, Roy Keely, J. R. Kerr, David Kinnamon, Jason Locy, Brad Lomenick, Evan Loomis, Ron Mahurin, Jena and James Nardella, David Neff, Ted Olsen, Katie Paris, Jon Passavant, Mark Rogers, Roger Sandberg, Read Schuchardt, Gideon Strauss, Baxter Underwood, Darren Whitehead and Kyle Young—and many more.

Frances Whitehead gets her own line for love and thanks.

My work required a great deal of travel, so the love of friends in Nashville kept me anchored: the church family at First Baptist Nashville, particularly Cliff and Mary Vaughan; the Vaughan/Boling Sunday school class; and Pastor Frank Lewis. I couldn't have done any of it without Travis and Holly Ables, Will and Tiffany Acuff, Todd and Rachel Johnson, Thunder and Emily Jones, and Skip and Timshel Matheney. Thanks, y'all.

I am grateful for my family's encouragement and support. With every day I appreciate my parents, John and Valerie, more and more—especially their peace work in the 1980s, which laid a foundation for my life. I hope I can do it justice. The loving example of my grandmother Lillian and my late grandfather, Valentine, continues to guide me. My sisters and brothers through blood and marriage have, to date, provided a trio of reasons—Selim Aycaner, Joshua Tomlinson and Will Beauchamp—that give me every reason to work for a better future. And I am particularly grateful to my mother-in-law, Chantal, who so generously and bravely shared her memories of her father for this book.

My wife, Natalie, is my best friend and most ardent supporter. She predicted my return to anti-nuclear activism long before I thought it was a possibility, and she urged me on despite the inherent risk in launching a new nonprofit venture. She has patiently endured endless comings and goings, and has joined me on the road when possible. And she continues to encourage and challenge me in equal measure, including in the writing and subsequent editing of these pages. There is no aspect of my life that is not more joyful because of her.

Penultimate thanks go to Jonathan Merritt, who proved a true friend at a critical point in this book's development. He volunteered his time, travel and expertise to help me corral and harness a wild, inchoate herd of ideas into a book with direction and intention. Jonathan lives his vocation as a writer as faithfully and passionately as anyone I know, and his counsel was as indispensable in the creation of these pages as his friendship has been to me personally. I am profoundly grateful to him.

Finally, this book is dedicated to two men whom it was my deepest privilege to know and to serve: Senator Alan Cranston (1914–2000) and the Reverend Dr. John R. W. Stott, CBE (1921–2011). These remarkable individuals could not have been more different from each other. One was a rather irreligious warhorse of American politics and the other a global evangelical statesman. But both had extraordinary integrity, bravery and purpose. My time with them has spurred me, as a young man, to think constantly about finishing well. I can only hope that I will do some honor to their loving example.

Soli Deo Gloria.

Tyler Wigg-Stevenson
Pentecost, A.D. 2012
Toronto, Canada

NOTES

Chapter 1: The World Is Not Ours to Save
[1] James Davison Hunter, *To Change the World* (Oxford: Oxford University Press, 2010), pp. 9ff.

Chapter 5: Take These Snakes
[1] "Israel and the Occupied Territories and the Palestinian Authority: Without distinction—attacks on civilians by Palestinian armed groups," Amnesty International, July 11 2002, accessed May 24, 2012, <http://www.unhcr.org/refworld/docid/3d2eea8e4.html>.

Chapter 6: The Peaceable Kingdom
[1] See also Matthew 5:9; Mark 9:50; Luke 10:5; Romans 12:18; 14:17, 19-20; 16:20; 1 Corinthians 7:15; 2 Corinthians 13:11; Galatians 5:22; Ephesians 2:17; 6:15; Colossians 3:15; 1 Timothy 2:2; 2 Timothy 2:22; Titus 3:2; Hebrews 12:11-14; James 3:17-18; and 1 Peter 3:11, among others.
[2] "John Piper—Make War," accessed December 20, 2011, <http://www.youtube.com/watch?v=wrYØh33coR4>.

Chapter 7: Peace with God
[1] History of Coventry Cathedral is taken from Michael Sadgrove, *Coventry Cathedral*, ed. John McIlwain (Norfolk, UK: Heritage House Group, 2009), pp. 4-7.
[2] BBC, "1940: Germans bomb Coventry to destruction," *On This Day* website, accessed December 12, 2012, <http://news.bbc.co.uk/onthisday/hi/dates/stories/november/15/newsid_3522000/3522785.stm>.
[3] "Why Coventry?" Coventry International Prize for Peace and Reconciliation, accessed December 12, 2012, <http://coventrypeaceprize.org.uk/?page_id=7>.
[4] Sadgrove, *Coventry Cathedral*, p. 10.

Chapter 8: Peace Among the Nations
[1] Bruce Waltke, "Righteousness in Proverbs," *Westminster Theological Journal* 70 (2008): 236.
[2] Ibid.
[3] Jared Diamond, "What's Your Consumption Factor?" *New York Times*, January 2, 2008, p. A17.
[4] "Background paper on SIPRI military expenditure data, 2010," Stockholm International Peace Research Institute, pp. 2-3, accessed December 18, 2011, <http://www.sipri.org/research/armaments/milex/factsheet2010>.
[5] Quoted material comes from personal correspondence with Dave Kiersznowski, as well as a talk by Dave at Laity Lodge, Texas, April 16, 2011. Audio accessed De-

cember 18, 2011, and available at <http://www.laitylodge.org/retreat-on-vocation-april-2011>.

[6]Andrew Bacevich, "Was the Iraq War Worth It?," Council on Foreign Relations Expert Roundup, December 15, 2011, accessed December 18, 2011, <http://www.cfr.org/iraq/iraq-war-worth-/p26820>.

[7]By late 2011, drone attacks had killed 175 Afghani and Pakistani children. "Number of CIA drone strikes in Pakistan hits 300," Bureau of Investigative Journalism, accessed December 18, 2011, <http://www.thebureauinvestigates.com/2011/10/14/grim-milestone-as-300th-cia-drone-strike-hits-pakistan>.

Chapter 9: Peace in Community
[1]C. J. H. Wright, "Family," *Anchor Bible Commentary,* vol. 2, ed. David Noel Freedman (New York: Doubleday, 1992), p. 765.
[2]Karl Barth, *The Epistle to the Romans,* trans. E. Hoskyns (New York: Oxford, 1968), p. 37.

Chapter 10: Living Out Our Callings
[1]As quoted by a study assistant predecessor, John Yates III, in "Pottering and Prayer," *Christianity Today,* April 2001, accessed December 30, 2011, <http://www.christianitytoday.com/ct/2001/april2/4.60.html>.

ABOUT THE AUTHOR

Tyler Wigg-Stevenson (B.A. Swarthmore College, M.Div. Yale University Divinity School) is the founding director of the Two Futures Project, a movement of American Christians for the abolition of nuclear weapons that has been recognized by secular and religious media including PBS, *Christianity Today* and *The Washington Post*, and which was also named by *Relevant Magazine* as one of "50 Ideas that Changed Everything." Tyler also chairs the Global Task Force on Nuclear Weapons, an initiative of the World Evangelical Alliance, and is a contributing editor to *Sojourners* magazine. He is the author of *Brand Jesus: Christianity in a Consumerist Age* (Seabury), as well as numerous book chapters and articles, which have received awards from the Associated Church Press and the Evangelical Press Association. Tyler and his wife, a theologian, live in Toronto, where he fills his spare time with doctoral studies, service as the associate pastor of an eclectic urban parish, and Thai kickboxing.

www.tylerws.com
www.twofuturesproject.org
Facebook: http://facebook.com/twofuturesproject
Twitter: @tylerws
     @2FP

LIKEWISE. *Go and do.*

A man comes across an ancient enemy, beaten and left for dead. He lifts the wounded man onto the back of a donkey and takes him to an inn to tend to the man's recovery. Jesus tells this story and instructs those who are listening to "go and do likewise."

Likewise books explore a compassionate, active faith lived out in real time. When we're skeptical about the status quo, Likewise books challenge us to create culture responsibly. When we're confused about who we are and what we're supposed to be doing, Likewise books help us listen for God's voice. When we're discouraged by the troubled world we've inherited, Likewise books encourage us to hold onto hope.

In this life we will face challenges that demand our response. Likewise books face those challenges with us so we can act on faith.

ivpress.com/likewise
twitter.com/likewise_books
facebook.com/likewisebooks
youtube.com/likewisebooks